ALAIN PROST

ALAIN PROST

MAURICE HAMILTON

BLINK
bringing you closer

CONTENTS

FOREWORD

Despite all his success, I don't think Alain Prost has been given the credit he deserves for his glittering Formula 1 career.

After all, this is a man who won 51 World Championships Grands Prix, achieving victories with marques as famous as McLaren, Ferrari, Williams and Renault and four world titles – a tally only beaten by the great Juan Manuel Fangio and Michael Schumacher.

But the numbers are only a small part of the story. I think Alain is one of those pivotal drivers in the history of Formula 1 – one whose style and focus redefined how we think of a Grand Prix driver; who forced other drivers to adapt and change in order to beat him. The greats like Fangio, Stewart, Lauda, Senna and Schumacher all brought an extra layer of application and intensity to the art of driving a race car – and you can easily add Alain to that list.

His ability to think deeply about the nuances of set-up and his style of using minimal, precise inputs to place his machinery under the least amount of mechanical stress gave him a considerable edge over his competitors.

Those skills were also something that his chief rival Ayrton Senna studied and adopted in his personal quest to beat the Frenchman. Equally, when I was growing up and cutting my teeth in karting, I too made no secret of my desire to emulate Alain's smooth and

sympathetic driving style – it just made sense. It no doubt helped that it looked effortlessly cool, too!

People say you should never meet your heroes as they never live up to your expectations, but Alain does. During my career, I feel so lucky to have spent time with Alain, learning about his approach to driving and racing, and I feel extremely proud whenever I'm compared to him.

Incredibly, it's been 30 years since Alain won his first world title in one of those iconic red and white McLarens – an achievement which the publication of this book celebrates – but he remains as knowledgeable and committed to Formula 1 as he ever did – and long may that continue.

Jenson Button
May 2015

UNIROYAL

BREIT REGENREIFEN

Agip
Agip

LONGINE

PROLOGUE

These days, future Formula 1 stars seem to be marked out from the moment they can walk, never mind drive. Careers designed to lead to greatness are launched as soon as parents can either build or buy a kart for their budding Lewis Hamilton or Fernando Alonso. By the age of eight, the acolytes are racing and looking the part in miniature versions of the overalls and helmets worn by their heroes.

In March 2015, the F1 bar was raised – or lowered, in terms of age – when Max Verstappen took part in a Grand Prix at the age of 17, the youngest to do so. He had reached the highest level of motor sport before he had barely left school. And yet it seemed perfectly normal.

How times have changed. Compare this to the early days of someone who was to become one of the most successful and admired drivers in the history of motor racing.

No one in their right mind, least of all the man himself, would have suggested Alain Prost was destined for sporting stardom at the start of his career. The little guy barely out of his teens, with chewed fingernails and a diffident demeanour, looked like a penniless apprentice jockey rather than a man who would establish records while winning 51 Grands Prix and four World Championships.

He seemed more likely to receive a parking ticket than the *Légion d'Honneur* and an OBE for services to British and French motor sport. No one would have said the nervy little fellow with the distinctive aquiline nose would charm women the world over as readily as race victories would succumb to his unique and gentle touch at the wheel.

Least of all, no one would have believed that this modest son of a furniture maker in the Loire would become embroiled in one of the most intense sporting rivalries ever known, as he fought wheel-to-wheel with the mercurial Ayrton Senna.

How could that be? Here was a Frenchman on a weekend pass from national service, driving a beat-up Renault and appearing to be going nowhere in particular. But Alain Marie Pascal Prost was heading south on the first stage of a path that would eventually take him to the top of the world. The fact that he was already 20, barely started in racing and would need to borrow a pair of overalls would be completely insignificant on the autumnal morning of Saturday 25 October in 1975.

These may have been very different days but the target was exactly as it is now. Prost's methods of getting there were to make a compelling story.

1. PUNCHING ABOVE HIS WEIGHT

The 1975 Grand Prix season had long since finished by Saturday 25 October but, for Alain Prost, his motor racing career was just beginning. The Formula 1 World Championship had been won by Niki Lauda; the first for the Austrian. His third and final world title would come nine years later at the end of an intense, season-long battle with his McLaren team-mate; the same driver who, for now, was focussed on gaining an important foothold on the bottom rung of the ladder. And typically, as the F1 world would later discover, Alain Prost was not averse to boxing clever while quietly exploiting every advantage on this October weekend.

The Winfield racing school, backed by Renault and Elf as a means of discovering future talent, had been established at two circuits; Magny-Cours near Nevers in central France and Paul Ricard between Toulon and Marseilles on the Mediterranean coast. Magny-Cours and Paul Ricard held identical competitions. The best 20 pupils at each school would take part in semi-finals held over two days, the top five moving forward to the final at each track in a bid to become Pilote Elf and, with it, a car to contest the Formula Renault Championship the following year. It was the ultimate prize. Winning the Pilote Elf was the sole aim of any young driver, particularly in France.

Although Prost lived with his parents in Saint Chamond, a small town much closer to Magny-Cours than Paul Ricard, he chose the latter because the weather was likely to be more favourable in the south of France. But it was an unseasonal shower that would allow Alain to show the first sign of an outstanding talent. Until that moment, he had remained quiet – timid, almost – as he went about his schooling – neat and tidy but not sensationally quick. And then the rain arrived.

Given the predominantly dry climate, the Paul Ricard track was heavily coated with a mix of dust, rubber and oil. Add a sprinkling of water and the surface would become abnormally slick. Several drivers spun off. But not Prost. That was notable in itself but the instructors were amazed and then impressed when the previously unnoticed pupil continued to brake at the same points used in the dry and yet negotiate the corners without drama. It was the first hint of an intuitive sense of feel and self-assurance that would make Alain Prost an outstanding driver of his generation and, arguably, one of the best ever. The point was not lost on Simon de Lautour, a leading instructor at the school.

Simon de Lautour

The entire course would have been held over seven or eight days. Depending on their time and finances – for a lot of the pupils it was quite expensive – they would often do a couple of days at a time. Very rarely did they do the course in one hit. Right from the start, Alain was discreet, but we began to see signs that he was naturally quick; that episode in the wet is a good example.

Looking at the technical side of Alain's driving from an instructor's point of view watching from the outside, he turned in very early. We had a particular teaching method because we had to adapt to cars that didn't have wide tyres. Alain was one of the first pupils we had who naturally carried his braking into the corner – and this went against the basics of everything we taught.

We had to develop our teaching programme on the basis of having to work around the average pupil. Of course, towards the end, if a pupil had a real talent you could start to teach them more individually. But to start off, it was a case of teaching the conventional method on the approach to a turn – where you brake and down change, come off the brakes and turn into the corner. The top drivers in F1, even in those early days, would carry their brakes into the turn. That's where Alain was really quite outstanding. Normally, by turning in early your exit isn't always that clean because you're tightening it up, but he was able to smooth that out every time. It was this intelligent approach that helped him stand out even though he was very, very unspectacular.

Alain Prost

I kept a low profile deliberately as I didn't want to draw attention to myself and show the opposition what the likely target would be. I noticed, for instance, that by exiting wide from a quick left-hander and going over a rumble strip, I gained maybe 100 to 200 revs on the following straight. I discovered that quite by chance but made sure I didn't let anyone else know. I wanted to save this for the final so that I could arrive fully charged and ready for an all-out attack. Of course, I had to get there first…

Prior to the Winfield racing school, Prost's experience had been limited to karts.

Prost comfortably qualified among the 20 semi-finalists and was through to the shoot-out that would determine the final five to make the final on 25 October. With competitors split into two groups of ten, Prost wanted to size up the opposition and the quality of single-seaters designed and manufactured by Martini to an identical specification. But, as Prost knew only too well, some would be more equal than others due to the harsh wear and tear of racing school life.

He was not best pleased to be drawn among the first group and told to report at 8:00 am on the Saturday. He arrived late, saying he had a puncture. It was not true. But the little white lie meant a switch to Sunday and an opportunity to note that the red Martini No 4 appeared to be marginally better than the rest.

Simon de Lautour

We accepted the fact that he might have had a puncture, although we also knew it could have been an excuse. In all fairness to our teaching methods, we did obviously allow for a discrepancy in the cars; it's very difficult to have six or seven cars identical. It's easy to understand from a pupil's point of view, from a morale point of view, why you would want to be in what appeared to be the best car. It was only later on when you realised what sort of driver Alain grew into that I was able to accept that the puncture story might not be true and with fair reason. That was clearly the way the man thought – even in those early days.

Prost's calculating mind and nascent talent would contribute to a place among the five finalists.

Simon de Lautour

Once we had chosen our five finalists we then set up a training programme with them that was provided free by the school so that they could put on a good performance. They did quite a lot of laps and some of the pupils were complaining about a gearbox we were using in those cars. In those days – which is amazing when you think about the semi-automatic gearboxes today – we actually taught pupils to double-declutch. Very few pupils actually did it because the Renault gearboxes were synchromesh but not brilliant gearboxes because they were straight out of a road car. To give the gearbox some possibility of lasting, we taught the pupils to double-declutch – which would normally help them in later years when they were going through Hewland gearboxes and so on which weren't synchromesh.

I tried the cars and had no problem with the gearbox so I asked them if they were double-declutching properly. They assured me they were. But to them, double-declutching was just blipping the throttle on the down-change. So I got them all into one of our Renault vans and we went round the track and I said show me how you double-declutch – and none of them, Alain included, did it properly.

In the meantime, Prost had a logistical detail to take care of. He was, coincidentally, doing national service at a barracks in Trier in the Rhineland. His limited number of weekend passes had already been accounted for by the racing school classes and competitions, leaving no allowance for the all-important day out on Saturday 25 October. By good fortune, Alain had been assigned to the adjutant's office. Finding the appropriate form and rubber stamp was the work of a furtive moment. (Not that he needed to worry. The colonel commanding the regiment would later write a letter of congratulations to the newly-crowned World Champion and reveal he was aware that his subordinate's deft touch at the wheel had been matched many years before by a sleight of hand with army paperwork.)

The importance of the Pilote Elf final could be judged by the attendance of Jean-Marie Balestre, the president of the Fédération Internationale du Sport Automobile (FISA), fulfilling his role with the world governing body as well as openly promoting young drivers 'pour la gloire de la France' – for the glory of France. Didier Pironi, Pilote Elf winner in 1972, flew down from Paris and was joined by French journalists and Pironi's future employer, Ken Tyrrell, the owner of the eponymous F1 team who would chair the judging panel.

The significant motor racing assembly added to the sense of occasion and could have aggravated a surprising error when Prost forgot to bring his overalls. He borrowed a light-blue suit from an instructor of a similarly slight build. It was well-worn and oversized, not that it made the slightest difference to what was to follow.

Simon de Lautour

The drivers normally went off on nine or ten laps to give them four warm-up laps before the clocks would start at the beginning of their first of five timed laps. It was worked out as an average lap time but obviously the fastest lap did count. I think the jury was always impressed by the fastest lap although clearly the average over the five laps was pretty important as well. But, really, it was the jury's decision with Ken Tyrrell as president.

Winning the Pilote Elf final was an incredible step up for these young drivers. They didn't all make F1 – it's a bit like wine; not every year is a classic – but if the driver had any talent, Elf were very good with them. In France, the standard procedure was you go to the Winfield school and go in for the Elf competition. So we had a lot of talented kids come to the school, which obviously helped us promote our product. I remember Ken saying there was not a more intense moment in a racing driver's career than this, because those five timed laps could make or break them.

Over a sequence of laps on the 2.2 km school circuit at one end of the Grand Prix track, Prost put the title beyond doubt with a lap time of 58.8 seconds. His nearest rival recorded a lap of 59.10 seconds. The remaining three took longer than 60 seconds. Ken Tyrrell, towering over the pint-sized winner, presented the cup.

'My team was sponsored by Elf at the time,' recalled Tyrrell many years later. 'Prost was outstanding, as I suppose you'd expect with the benefit of what we know now but, on that day, it was a walkover; he looked an absolute natural. Prost didn't really speak any English, and my French is non-existent, so I didn't really talk to him. I just gave him the trophy and then got to the airport to get home as quickly as I could.'

Tyrrell might have added that his beloved football team, Tottenham Hotspur, were playing Leicester City in what was then League One of the English Football League and he was keen to discover the result (Spurs won 3–2). Had Tyrrell been able to converse with Prost, they could have discussed a mutual love of football. Ken played as a youth for his village team while Prost was a keen participant in schoolboy soccer and avid follower of Saint Etienne, his local team. Indeed, football could have played an important part in his life had events not followed a particular course one day in the summer of 1970.

Tyrrell presents Prost with the Pilote Elf trophy at Paul Ricard on 25 October 1975. Jean-Marie Balestre, President of FISA, is over Tyrrell's left shoulder. Leading French journalist Gerard 'Jabby' Crombac (with pipe) and Simon de Lautour (extreme right) look on.

In the early summer of 1970 (the year Prost was to discover karting), Jochen Rindt won the
Monaco Grand Prix. The Austrian's Lotus leads Piers Courage in the De Tomaso (entered by
Frank Williams) and the March of Jo Siffert. In the background, the orange McLaren of Bruce
McLaren, the team Prost would ultimately drive for in a relatively less dangerous era for F1.
All four drivers in the picture would be dead within 18 months; two of them, Courage and
McLaren, in a matter of weeks.

Alain Marie Pascal Prost had been born 15 years before on 24 February 1955 in Saint-Chamond in the Loire department of the Rhône-Alpes region. His father, André, a calm and easy-going man, used a basement workshop at home to make tubes and, among other items, kitchen furniture. His mother, Marie-Rose, ran the typical family home in Rue Dugas-Montbel with quiet authority. Prost described life with his parents and older brother Daniel as 'happy and uncomplicated'.

Part of the pleasure was derived from time spent in a small holiday home on the Côte d'Azur. Noting one day in that summer of 1970 that his son was becoming bored with the beach and the sea, André took his offspring to the Siesta adventure playground between Antibes and Cannes. Among the attractions was a kart track.

Alain Prost

When I saw a go-kart for the first time, I did not know anything about it. For sure, I looked at the steering wheel and the seat and understood that – but I didn't know what to do. I'm not saying that I almost sat the wrong way round – but I was not interested at all. My brother was ill and we wanted to do all we could to make everything nice for him. While I was interested in football, Daniel was the one who would sit in my father's car and play with the knobs and the controls. I had no interest in that at all but, naturally, when he saw the go-karts, he wanted to have a go. I decided to go along with this because I wanted to do it for him. I wasn't thinking of myself and, besides, I had one arm in plaster because of a small accident I'd had.

But when I started to drive, it's something you cannot explain. That is very important because in life, you can have this kind of experience; it can be mental things, it can be physical, it can be painting or photography, I don't know what, but you think: 'That's for me.'

We had done ten minutes or something – it was a very short time – and I had this very good feeling. The guy said: 'Oh, because you have not done a lot, we can organise a sort of race together for another ten minutes.' I started at the back because of my arm and because I knew I would be driving with one hand. But I won the race.

The feeling I had was unbelievable. It was somehow being able to express yourself, of having your instincts take over, feelings you did not expect while doing something completely new. I always remember this day because it changed everything. I don't know if I would have been a professional football player – it was possible at the time because I was playing as an amateur and I was close to the club at Saint Etienne – but you can never tell.

All I know now is that the first moment in the kart was one of the most important moments of my life. And I say that having won all those races and championships; knowing everything I've been through and enjoyed. When you get a little older, you start to see things in a different way and I know I will never ever forget what happened on that day.

What happened next would be governed by the age-old obstacle in motor racing: money. Or, in Prost's case, the lack of it. That quickly became evident when he made enquiries at a small karting club at Rive de Gier, a few kilometres north-east of Saint-Chamond.

Alain Prost *I had to think of ways of raising money to buy a go-kart, which was obviously going to be difficult because I was still at school and working with my father in my spare time. When I told my parents I wanted to do this, they said, 'Forget it'. So, for a year and a half, I did everything I could to get some money. For example, every time I told my parents I was going to the cinema with my brother, he would go, tell me later what the film was all about and I would save the money. For 18 months, I never went to the cinema or night clubs; I didn't go anywhere. At Christmas, I said I didn't want any presents, just give me the money instead.*

I did lots of different things. A friend who had a furniture removal company was also doing some karting. I said I would work with him to earn money and help when he went karting – but I didn't want my parents to know. That's why they were surprised when, after a year and a half, I told them I had saved 700 [French] francs [approximately £50 in 1971] and I was going to buy a kart. Obviously, it was a second-hand engine and chassis. But I would be racing. The feeling of wanting to do it was as strong, if not stronger, than ever.

Prost did the majority of his racing at Rive de Gier, on a busy day joining about a hundred competitors categorised by engine type and split into races of 14 karts at a time. Initially, Prost made little impact as he found his feet and began to learn the craft while his parents watched from the sidelines. André Prost helped where he could but both father and son realised they did not have enough knowledge to work on the engine and make a difference.

Alain Prost *A guy in Paris, Michel Fabre, owned a company called Sovame which imported the best karts and engines on the market. I explained that I had no money but I wanted to learn about preparing engines. I told Michel I wanted to represent his company in my part of France and in return I could finance my season and also learn from him about engines and be a sort of works driver. Without an agreement like this, I would not be able to go racing. Michel had seen me race – he would become a big supporter of mine – and we agreed a deal. Every single day I worked on the chassis and engine until 1:00 or 2:00 am, knowing I was going to school at 7:00am the following morning.*

The arrangement with Michel was unusual in those days but it was a fantastic help for me. I was able to persuade my parents that I could become a professional and they gave their blessing for me to leave school a year ahead of the final form in 1973.

Prost would find it difficult to resist getting behind the wheel of a kart following his retirement from F1. He drives a French Sodi Kart at Longchamp in November 1996 (above) and takes part in the Karting Masters at Bercy in December 1993 (overleaf).

Prost ran a Vacquand kart, the improved performance from the French chassis helping him win the French and the European Junior Championships in 1973 before moving up to take the senior European title 12 months later. The earnings allowed Prost to consider attending the racing school at Paul Ricard in 1975. But he was not yet done with karting. In fact, Alain was to leave an impression in every sense when, uniquely over his entire career, he came to blows with another driver.

The race in question was the Alazar Trophy, a prestigious event held near Paris. The favourite was François Goldstein, a Belgian racer several years older than Prost. Goldstein was not afraid to get involved in controversial incidents, as others such as the UK's Terry Fullerton would attest – the 1973 World Champion (later the driver Ayrton Senna admired most) having been driven off the road by Goldstein at an important final the previous year.

Prost won three heats and the first final, the second being decisive. He led the first 18 laps. With two laps remaining, he was forced off by Goldstein's team-mate. Alain rejoined behind Goldstein and watched the Belgian win outright. On the slowing down lap, Prost repaid the opposition team's tactic, the two karts coming to a standstill at the outside of the first corner – where Prost promptly jumped from his machine and punched Goldstein on the throat (they were wearing open-face crash helmets).

Alain Prost *This is true – and I don't regret it. This was a day when I realised a lot of things about life, not just racing. In the part of France I came from, things like education and family values were based on hard work and justice. I was not prepared for what happened in this race. It might have been different if I had come from Paris or another big city where the values are not the same. But, for me, the background was remembering my grandfather, mother and father working like hell for everything we had. My thinking was based on that. The Alazar Trophy was really a very special day and I would be competing against Goldstein, who had won the World Championship a couple of times. He was the man we all wanted to beat.*

I was first in qualifying, won the heats and the first final. In go-karting it's the second final that counts because, if you win the first and finish second in the next one, it's the second one that counts. I had won everything and was leading by ten seconds. I was the best; I was the fastest. Goldstein's team-mate was one lap behind. He waited for me and pushed me out. By the time I got started again, Goldstein was ahead, it was the last lap and there was nothing I could do.

I was so furious. When Goldstein crossed the line, he just gave me his hand, you know, to shake hands. I could not accept that. Going down the straight, I pushed him right off the road at the first corner. He was a lot taller than me – but we had a big fight. I'm not proud of it but, if I had to do it again, I would.

I also realised for the first time that, despite having something obvious like that happen on the track, you can never have 100 per cent of the people behind you. I began to understand that was the case even though, in this instance, we were in France, close to Paris, and yet the people watching were 50:50 about who was at fault. I've always kept this what you might call 'souvenir' in my mind.

When I talked to Goldstein about it many years later, we laughed. But at the time it was very serious, not just winning from a personal point of view but also because we were each representing different manufacturers and it was very important for them to win as well. That was the first time I was able to consistently beat the best driver in the world. I have always detested poor sportsmanship. As a result, I could not accept what happened on the track. Not at all.

The karting officials could not accept the sight of one driver punching another. Prost received a six-month ban from racing for his trouble. Time spent on the bench in the early part of the 1975 season did not blunt his competitive edge. If anything, it made him even more hungry, as proved by more victories and a second French senior championship at the end of the year.

This was important for reasons other than getting back on track: the new title brought with it a scholarship, followed by Prost's decision to attend the Renault-Elf Winfield school at Paul Ricard and his brief but significant encounter with Ken Tyrrell on 25 October 1975.

Elf used their sponsorship of the Tyrrell F1 team to have Ken Tyrrell assist with oil company promotions, particularly Pilote Elf. Tyrrell assumes his usual commanding position at the pit wall.

2. SWEET MARTINI

Despite winning Pilote Elf in 1975, Prost had never taken part in a motor race. The curious anomaly was created by the Winfield school focussing on driving technique rather than race craft. He may have gained plenty of the latter in karting but Prost was only too aware that racing a Martini-Renault Mk17 would be very different.

His gleaming prize, a neat and relatively simple single-seater powered by a four-cylinder Renault engine, came with enough funds to run the car in the French Championship. This dream didn't turn into the nightmare commonly created by the many vagaries of motor sport – uncompetitive chassis, down-on-power engine, mechanical failures, being taken out by other drivers, sheer bad luck – as Prost won every race bar one.

The failure – if you could call it that – came in the final race of 13, which meant Alain was already 1976 Formula Renault Champion; not that you would have known it judging by his downbeat expression at an end-of-season party thrown by Renault and Elf. He may have dominated his rivals (including Frederic Watelet, who had won the parallel Pilote Elf at Magny-Cours in 1975) but Prost was deeply frustrated that ignition trouble had denied a clean sweep; a competitive characteristic that would drive him through the difficulties in seasons to come. (Watelet, having come second to Prost more times than he cared to mention that season, quit motor sport and went off to run a pub.)

Prost knew Formula Renault Europe, with its more powerful engine and wider tyres, would provide the next step on the ladder. Indeed, he had already gained a foothold in 1976 when invited to race a Lola in the championship round at Dijon.

Prost starts from pole at Paul Ricard (previous page) and goes on to score one of his many Formula Renault victories in 1976 in the Martini-Renault Mk17.

Alain Prost

I'd already won three rounds of the Formula Renault championship in 1976 when I was asked to race with the Danielson Renault Europe team [alongside Richard Dallest and Alain Cudini] at Dijon. I had no hesitation in doing this because all the top guys who had done well in Formula Renault in previous seasons were there. I remember I was on pole for my qualifying heat – which I won – and that meant I started from the front row alongside Didier Pironi, who had won the other heat. Something happened to my car at the start and I was down the field [ninth] at the end of the first lap. I was very keen to do well and I went for it, moving up to second place behind Pironi. Then my engine lost all its oil and that was it.

Not that it mattered by this stage, but someone had protested my engine because they thought that was the reason for my performance. That would not be the last time another driver or team would be suspicious simply because they had been beaten. I didn't worry about it too much because I thought I had done enough to impress the right people.

Among them was François Guiter. A large man with a quiet presence, Guiter had been hired by Elf in 1967 to promote the French state petro-chemical company.

François Guiter

I was in charge of the launch in 1967. Basically Elf was a technical company run by engineers. They were very good at what they did – deep-sea drilling and so on – but they didn't know how to go about marketing their company. They said they wanted to become associated with products for automobiles and be involved on the technical side. So I was wondering what would be a link between the technical aspect and the general public. The problem was that at that time France was nowhere in motor racing. Apart from the success of Alpine in rallying, there was nothing. We needed to look at F1 and something that would be a potential winner.

I WAS VERY KEEN TO DO WELL AND I WENT FOR IT, MOVING UP TO SECOND PLACE BEHIND PIRONI. THEN MY ENGINE LOST ALL ITS OIL AND THAT WAS IT.
ALAIN PROST

The link with F1 would come through Matra (the French aerospace company that also made racing cars) and then Tyrrell, but not before Guiter had established Elf in the junior formulae to help promote both his company and future French drivers, Pilote Elf being a classic example. Having watched Prost progress, Guiter was prepared to listen to a suggestion from his young protégé.

Alain Prost

François Guiter had always been strongly involved because he represented Elf and he was taking care of the programme for young drivers, bringing them to F1. You could say that, without him, Renault would not have come to F1 in 1977 because Elf, not Renault, paid for the turbo programme [the first turbo engine to appear in contemporary F1]. He was pushing Renault all the way. I remember talking with him at the time about the racing drivers' school and all that it brings and he said, in 30 years, we will remember that Elf was there from the beginning, bringing drivers to F1. And he was right. It cost Elf a lot of money but it was a very big help to drivers like me.

Simon De Lautour

Elf used motor racing as the way to launch its product. It was a relatively young company, younger than the Winfield school in fact, and used motor racing in general as its platform. There wasn't a single French racing driver throughout the mid-1960s and the 1970s, perhaps even beyond, who didn't at some point go through Elf.

François Guiter was a super bloke. He'd go up to people in the F1 pits and say 'I want you to try this driver' – and they'd jump to it. He had a lot of charisma and a lot of clout. We were all in awe of him at the start.

Alain Prost

François Guiter and I would become very close over the years and it was always a pleasure to see him. Motor sport needs people like him – the type of guy who can handle different relationships. It's never easy between French and English people but, when it works, it works very well. French people have a different mentality – but Guiter was not like French people. That's why I liked him and felt able to talk to him. I was very sad when he passed away at the end of 2014.

Normally, when you win Pilote Elf, you become part of a team. I went to François Guiter and asked if it was possible for him to give me the budget to run my own team. You only needed two mechanics for a Formula Renault team and I wanted to handle my own budget rather than be integrated into a team. He said, 'If you win the championship, you have a budget for the year after. If you don't win the championship – it's finished.'

That was pressure straight away but I won the championship [in 1976], so I had the budget for the year after. I needed to find some more money but, basically, I had my own team for Formula Renault Europe in 1977.

Before moving up to Formula 3 with the Martini-Renault Mk27 in 1979 (previous page), Prost had a brief taste of Formula 2 in 1978 driving a Chevron-Hart B40 entered by Fred Opert. He retired with engine failure after starting from the third row at Pau.

If Formula Renault in 1976 had been a comparative stroll, 1977 would be a slog. Prost was up against Dany Snobeck, Jean-Louis Bousquet and Jacques Coulon; drivers with Formula Renault Europe experience who felt they now had to win the title or, at the very least, not be beaten by the upstart, Prost. Snobeck won four races on the trot, including the prestigious round supporting the Monaco Grand Prix. Prost retaliated with victories at Nogaro and Magny-Cours, only for Bousquet to throw his hat into the ring with three wins, Coulon then making his claim with two. By winning two of the last three, Prost ensured he was the favourite going into the final round at Paul Ricard. Bousquet won but a typically measured drive into seventh place ensured Prost was able to beat his former karting rival by three points.

Alain Prost *I remember 1977 very well because it was a struggle, both technically and physically. It was nothing like 1976, which had seemed very nice and simple by comparison. This was difficult because I was running my own team and the competition was very strong all the way to the end of the season. I had won six races with a lot of fastest laps and pole positions and the good thing was I had been racing outside France on tracks such as Hockenheim, Zolder and Monza. I thought it would be good experience for whatever was to come in 1978.*

Inbetween successful seasons in Formula Renault and Formula 3, Prost had a difficult time in 1977 with the Martini-Renault Mk20.

Prost was undecided which way to move – stay in Formula Renault Europe for another season, step up to Formula 3 or leap into Formula 2. Having persuaded Renault Sport to adapt their V6 engine for F2 and F1, Guiter talked the manufacturer into building a F3 unit based on the Renault 20TS four-cylinder engine. It would be installed in a Martini Mk21B and run by ORECA, a team owned by Hugues de Chaunac.

Having raced in largely domestic formulae, Prost jumped into the deep end of international motor sport. The European F3 Championship was hugely competitive with, for example, no fewer than 108 drivers entering the Monza Lottery, a classic event on the famous autodrome. Miffed to have lost out on one victory in 1976, Prost counted himself lucky to gain a single win (at Jarama in Spain) in 1978. In truth, the Martini-Renault package was not yet competitive in a field dominated by the finely-honed Ralts, Chevrons and March chassis powered by Toyota engines.

Jan Lammers was crowned European F3 Champion in 1978. The Dutchman had scraped home by the finest of margins after a lengthy battle with Anders Olofsson, a seasoned Swedish driver who decided to reduce his involvement the following year. As Olofsson backed off, Martini and Renault picked up pace, just as Guiter had hoped they would. Olofsson and Prost would have one more interesting confrontation at Knutsdorp, Olofsson's home race.

Olofsson would later quit F3 and go on to win three consecutive Japanese touring car titles and the Spa 24 Hours as well as gaining respectable results in international sports car racing. He retired from racing at the end of 1997 and died at the age of 55 in 2008. Recalling that race at Knutsdorp on 5 August 1979, Olofsson would give a revealing insight. Going into the first corner, Prost's Martini had been hit hard enough to buckle the front wheel. Despite the obvious upset to the handling, Prost worked his way back to second place and closed on Olofsson's three-year-old Ralt.

Anders Olofsson

In 1979, I was only doing F3 occasionally. I knew Knutsdorp very well and was actually leading when Prost suddenly out-braked me at the end of the straight. I was ten, maybe 15 metres in front and I didn't expect him to dive for the corner from that far back. He controlled me a little bit. He braked so bloody late and came on to my inside and then I realised it was too late to close the door – but that showed his judgement and balance with the car.

I remember this very clearly because you do expect the person behind to try an out-braking manoeuvre but I was watching in my mirror and I simply didn't expect it at that moment. I thought he was too far behind. What he's got is a total balance. His body tells him – his body gives him better information than the average good racing driver about where the limits are and how to drive quickly, not only in late braking but taking the corner at high speed and getting a good exit. It's a combination of many things, of course, but it is his car balance which seems to be so exceptional. That was evident at Knutsdorp, a difficult circuit for any foreign driver, but he didn't have any problems with that. When he is behind the steering wheel, the whole package is so complete: he is aggressive but in control, he doesn't do desperate things and that's another of his strengths.

By the time of that race, Prost was the man to beat, having won five of the eight races. But the great and the good of Grand Prix racing had already seen enough, particularly when Prost had totally dominated the Monaco F3 race in May. His subsequent crowning as

1979 European F3 Champion merely rubber-stamped the approval. Getting results and recognition was one thing; converting that into a F1 drive would be quite another. Keen to put himself about, Prost went to the Dutch Grand Prix on 26 August and was slightly taken aback by his reception – or lack of it.

Alain Prost

I was about to win the F3 championship but I was in for a shock. Everyone was civil but they couldn't really have cared who I was. They were busy going F1 racing – which, of course, is how it is. Luckily, François Guiter was there as usual and he introduced me to a few F1 people. The only possibilities for anything happening were with Fittipaldi and McLaren – and they weren't exactly the best at the time. [McLaren would finish seventh in the Constructors' Championship; Fittipaldi, 12th and last] I'd previously had contact with Ligier [third in the championship] and also with Marlboro [team sponsor of McLaren and personal sponsor of several drivers]. In fact, after I won in Monaco, John Hogan and Patrick ['Paddy'] McNally from Marlboro talked to me and that

would lead to an interesting situation at the end of the season.

Once I had won the F3 title, François Guiter suggested I should go to the last two Grands Prix in Canada [Montreal] and the USA [Watkins Glen], so I travelled with two French journalist friends, Eric Bhat [Grand Prix International] and Jean-Louis Moncet [L'Auto Journal]. I spoke with Paddy and John in Canada and also Teddy Mayer [boss of McLaren] and there was talk of a drive in Watkins Glen. At the same time, Niki Lauda suddenly left Brabham in the middle of practice in Montreal and I had a discussion with Bernie [Ecclestone, owner of Brabham] about taking Niki's place. I found myself in this strange situation where I suddenly had a few doors opening – and this was as well as Elf, because François Guiter wanted me to go to Ligier.

THAT FEELING ONLY GREW WHEN, ON A BEAUTIFUL DAY IN THE SOUTH OF FRANCE, I SAT IN A F1 CAR AND HELD THE STEERING WHEEL FOR THE FIRST TIME.
ALAIN PROST

Jean-Louis Moncet

We were not what you might call close friends in the beginning; just journalists keeping an eye on French drivers and being aware of what Prost had been doing in F3 and, before that, Formula Renault. When he came with Eric and me to the USA, I remember he had no money; he was not a rich boy. Eric and I were sharing a room and we said, 'You're a small guy; you don't take up much room! You can share with us.' He was very easy to get along with and we could see that he was getting into some confusion over what to do about the F1 drives he suddenly had on offer.

Alain Prost

I was quite interested in Brabham, and McLaren too but I didn't know what to do. Brabham took [Ricardo] Zunino and in the end I said, 'No' to Marlboro. I asked them to understand that I didn't want to make a mistake; I didn't know Watkins Glen and I didn't know the car. I said I thought it would be a better idea to organise a test. I came back to France and waited for at least two weeks without any news. I was really feeling bad, thinking maybe I had blown my chance, that offers of F1 drives don't come very often. François Guiter tried to help me, which was nice, but he had no contact with Marlboro. It's at times like that when you begin to have nagging doubts. I had won a couple of championships but I didn't know if that was enough. I could only wait.

A month after Watkins Glen, Prost got the call. McLaren were in discussion about continuing with Patrick Tambay and they were looking at other prospective partners for John Watson. McLaren said they would give Prost a test along with the American driver Kevin Cogan, at Paul Ricard in early November.

Alain Prost

Teddy was pushing for Kevin Cogan because they were both American and Cogan had been winning in Formula Atlantic [the North American equivalent of F2]. I think Patrick [Tambay] was still under consideration. Certainly, I did not feel I was the favourite in the beginning. But that did not matter because I was convinced I would do well, especially at Ricard. That feeling only grew when, on a beautiful day in the south of France, I sat in a F1 car and held the steering wheel for the first time. Initially it [the McLaren M29] seemed quite a big car. I did one slow lap and then one a little bit quicker and, on the third one, I said to myself, 'It's okay. I'm going to do it.' Without knowing the lap time, it felt good.

Prost's intuition was correct. Standing at the pit wall with McLaren crew chief Tyler Alexander, Mayer clicked his stopwatch as the red and white McLaren-Cosworth V8 accelerated out of the final corner. Watson had established a benchmark time while setting up the car. Within a handful of laps, Prost equalled the time and then bettered it. Mayer noted that Prost got sideways when exiting the tight corner early on but didn't lose time in the same way again.

The start of a warm relationship. John Watson passes on his thoughts and experience after Prost's first run with the F1 McLaren at Paul Ricard in November 1979.

Prost looks on as Teddy Mayer (left), John Watson and
Tyler Alexander (hidden) discuss the McLaren M29.

John Watson

Along with everyone else, I had become aware of Alain Prost through his efforts in F3, particularly winning at Monaco. The 1979 season had been one of McLaren's worst and they and Marlboro were looking to move forward and not continue with Patrick [Tambay]. McLaren felt they wanted to nominate their particular option – Kevin Cogan – and Marlboro were very keen on Prost.

I drove the car and then Cogan was given a go. Sometimes you get intuitive feelings about people or situations. When Kevin got in the car, I thought he was very nervous or he had no, what I would call, natural feel. He was crunching when getting gears; he went down the pit lane with the revs all over the place.

From the moment Alain got in the car, it was a different world. Everything seemed totally within his capacity, both mentally and physically. He had a sense of feel that Kevin didn't have. When he went down the pit lane, the gear changes were clean straight away. And, from there on, everything he did in the car marked him as being somebody a bit special.

Politically, it was a bone of contention between the two sides: Teddy [Mayer] and Marlboro, principally John Hogan. Marlboro felt they'd lost out because of Teddy's decision to go down the Patrick Tambay route. As a result, Marlboro felt that they'd lost access to Gilles Villeneuve for the '78 season because he had gone off and signed for Ferrari. Marlboro were not going to let The Wiener [Mayer's nickname among team members] impose yet again on their wishes. It was actually a no-brainer because Alain was clearly an outstanding young driver. While no one could fully appreciate what he might achieve, at this stage he was way ahead of Kevin Cogan.

John Hogan

I was essentially in charge of the motor racing programme at Philip Morris [Marlboro]. I used to comb the motor racing world because I thought that was the only way you could stay on top of the job. It was actually François Guiter who brought our attention to Prost. I was standing trackside watching the F3 race at Monaco when François sidled up to me and said, 'You know, 'e eez very good.' I still have a great faith in F3 as a proving ground and, at the time, I knew François was trying to push French drivers. I also had a little challenge in the back of my mind, in that I wanted to have the first French World Champion.

As a consequence, I kept an eye on Alain until the end of the 1979 season. I said to Paddy [McNally], who I was working with at the time, that we should really do something about that guy. But how? McLaren at that point were at their lowest possible ebb, I mean, just awful. They needed an injection of youthful driving talent, so we eased Prost into the McLaren at Ricard – and he was lightning from the word go. That test proved it.

Tyler Alexander

I'm not sure exactly how many laps Prost did but he was a reasonable amount quicker than John during his first run – which was pretty impressive for a first time out in a F1 car. When he came into the pits, Teddy had his clipboard ready. Prost thought it was the timing sheets to look at – actually, Teddy had already been to the boot of his car and got out a contract he wanted him to sign! That was more or less it. Alain Prost would be racing for McLaren in 1980.

Alain Prost finished sixth in his first Grand Prix in January 1980. As F1 debuts go, this was as impressive as it comes – particularly after starting from the middle of the grid with a difficult car and enduring 53 laps of the Buenos Aires Autodrome in torrid mid-summer heat.

Prost's M29B was a modified version of the 1979 Marlboro McLaren-Cosworth M29 he had driven for the first time just over a month before during the test at Paul Ricard. These days, F1 teams would not consider racing the previous year's car, even if the regulation changes calling for safety improvements allowed it.

The test had been all about lap time, staying error-free and making the best of the exciting opportunity. Now, in the relentlessly competitive atmosphere of a Grand Prix weekend in Argentina, novelty value for the driver and a degree of forbearance by the team was replaced by the urgent need for results from a car that was beginning to reveal its shortcomings to the novice. The extent of a handling imbalance would be demonstrated by John Watson qualifying 17th – although sympathy was diluted by the Ulsterman being almost a second slower than his new team-mate.

Watson had no chance to bring his experience to bear and make amends in the race when he retired, after five laps, with a gearbox oil leak. Prost, meanwhile, dropped a place on successive laps to Keke Rosberg (Fittipaldi-Cosworth), Gilles Villeneuve (Ferrari) and Elio de Angelis (Lotus-Cosworth) as he settled in and took stock of conditions that were becoming trickier by the lap. Number 15 Circuit in Parque Almirante Brown had been resurfaced but poor workmanship failed to cope with fat rear tyres and January heat. Within a handful of laps, the racing line was fringed by a mix of rubber and fine grit.

Alain Prost

It was like driving on packed ice with no grip at all. I obviously wanted to create a good impression with my first race and I could see that this was actually an opportunity. There was no way we could compete with Williams or Ligier or Brabham or any of the top teams, particularly with drivers who were more experienced. But it was obvious that there would be a lot of incidents on this track. My plan was just to drive as quickly but as carefully as I could in the conditions. I think I did have a spin at one point – so did most drivers – but I kept going.

Prost prepares to leave the pits in Argentina in the McLaren M29 during his first Grand Prix weekend in January 1980. Alain is about to fit the white pipe supplying oxygen to his helmet in the event of a fire.

There would be seven finishers from 24 starters at the end of a gruelling hour and 45 minutes. Never lower than tenth, Prost scored his first of an eventual career total of 798.5 championship points by finishing one lap behind the winning Williams-Cosworth of Alan Jones. The F1 establishment, particularly Renault-Elf, took note.

A fortnight later, Prost was worse off in qualifying (13th) but one better in the race when he put the stamp on his F1 debut by finishing fifth, this time at the bumpy and demanding Interlagos track in Brazil. The plan had been for another circumspect drive but Prost was forced to rely on hard lessons learned in karting when he caught the Arrows of Riccardo Patrese.

This was the start of Patrese's fourth F1 season, his reputation for being an aggressive driver underlined by several brutal moves as he fended off the novice in the McLaren. Prost remained remarkably calm and persistent before finally making a concise pass after 11 laps of probing and of being forced to back out of legitimate moves. It was his patience when dealing with such a forceful opponent as much as the ability to bring the car home that earned Prost more recognition. Watson, meanwhile, finished one lap down and six places behind.

John Watson

Alain was working with Teddy [Mayer] at this time. Teddy was a very good engineer from an era when you improved the car by messing around with springs, dampers, roll bars and so on. But we were moving into a period when that was... not irrelevant, but becoming much less important. The key to a car being competitive in 1980 was downforce, much as Ligier had done in '79 and then Williams and Brabham were doing in '80 by bringing much more sophisticated aerodynamic parts to the car. So, here we had a situation where I was saying the problems, in my view, were of an aerodynamic nature while, at the same time, Alain was getting more out of the car simply by going through the age-old process of roll bars and dampers with Teddy. He had arrived in F1 fresh and without being jaundiced by anything he had found in previous years. And, on top of all that, the guy was outstanding. There were no issues or questions about that. He was just bloody quick.

The growing problem for McLaren was fielding a car that appeared to be unlikely to do justice to the nascent talent of its young driver. The introduction of a longer bell housing and the need for swept-back front wishbones and revised suspension proved to be a step too far. During a midweek test at Kyalami prior to the third round in South Africa, a failure at the front of the car, now designated M29C, at the medium-speed right-hand bend at Leeukop sent Prost into a concrete wall (such close proximity of a wall to the track would never be allowed today).

Shaken but otherwise okay, Alain prepared himself for practice on the Thursday, the race to take place on Saturday. If he had the beginning of niggling concerns about the integrity of the M29C, those doubts would mushroom when he flew off the road once more – this time, it was the rear suspension – and hit the wall for a second time. Initially, it seemed he had got away without serious injury. But when a swollen left wrist became painful that evening, it was evident something needed to be done.

But this was 1980. There was little or no medical back-up. And neither, it seemed, was there anyone from the team to offer support and advice. Fortunately, however, Marie-Claude Beaumont, Renault's press officer, was staying in the same hotel as Prost.

Prost scored points in his first two Grands Prix in Argentina and Brazil.

Watson leads Prost near the back of the field during the
early laps of the Belgian Grand Prix. The McLaren pair
are ahead of Keke Rosberg, who would eventually finish
seventh in the Fittipaldi-Cosworth. Both McLarens would
run into technical trouble.

John Watson

Alain had gone off in the Esses and got whiplash through the steering wheel. When he complained of a really painful wrist, the attitude seemed to be, 'Oh, don't be such a tosser! You'll be all right for the race on Saturday.' Some time around 9:30–10:00 pm that night, I was about to go to my room and Marie-Claude Beaumont came after me and said, 'John! John! Alain is in agony. There's something wrong with his wrist and we can't get a doctor. Can you take him to hospital?'

I said she had to be joking; I was about to go to bed. She said they had looked for people from McLaren. There was no one around and I was the only person they could find. Alain was in some pain. There was nothing for it but to get him into my hire car and go look for the nearest hospital.

When we eventually found it, they took Alain away for an X-ray and he reappeared with a wrist in plaster and his arm in a sling! The doctor said he had broken his scaphoid, one of the smallest bones in your wrist and a really nasty one to break. When I asked if he could drive tomorrow they sort of looked at me and said, 'Impossible! He won't drive for six weeks.' Now it was my job, not just to get Alain back to the hotel but also to find The Weiner and break the bad news. Talk about the shit hitting the fan.

Alain Prost

John was like a big brother. He really didn't need to be so helpful because, obviously, I was beginning to make life difficult for him on the track. But he was always there with advice because, of course, he knew all the circuits and I didn't.

He never failed to pass on helpful information. It was so typical of John that he should take me to the hospital. The sad thing was that people were starting to say things about John – and things were happening in the team which I didn't feel very comfortable about. One of the guys – Tony Jardine, nicknamed 'Teach' – did cartoons and he drew one which made reference to me and John.

Tony Jardine

I had joined McLaren in 1980 and become a sort of assistant team manager to Teddy and Tyler [Alexander]. I had a little office upstairs at the factory in David Road, Colnbrook, right under the Heathrow flight path. You'd swear the wheels were touching the roof and when Concorde came over, you could forget about speaking on the phone for about five minutes; the noise was unbelievable.

My role was the administration of the team – flights, hotels, transport, imports, uniforms, all sorts of duties at the track. Bearing in mind that we were only a small team, we'd go testing in Brazil and Argentina at the beginning of the year, be away for six weeks and then go straight into races there. If something needed fixing, I'd go out and try to find parts or find a welder. I could be doing anything from sweeping the garage floor to helping lift a [Ford-Cosworth] DFV into the back of a chassis or going with Tyler to pick up suitcases of cruzeiros [then Brazilian currency] as prize money in Brazil! From the drivers' point of view, it was making sure their helmets and overalls were in place. There was a lot to do, be it running up to the stewards or fetching the timing sheets from the race office.

I'd seen Prost in F3 in 1979 and the next thing I knew we were giving him a test at Ricard. When the boys came back, they said he was very impressive. When he came in the factory for the first time, I really liked him. He was all that I had imagined he would be because I'd seen the pictures, read the reports, heard the stories. My feeling was that he was the right size and the right intensity. He was like a little jockey but we quickly decided that he was a little Napoleon and he earned the nickname 'Little Napper'. Some of the guys also christened him 'Tadpole' because of the French 'frog' link. In true McLaren style of the day, we had a tadpole sticker on the side of the car. He loved it.

When he came over to the factory or for testing and he didn't necessarily want to stay with Teddy, I'd pick him up from the

airport in my wife Jeanette's 2CV – the old Puddleduck. Being a Frenchman, he'd make rude remarks about it as we puttered along to his hotel. His wife – well, she was his girlfriend when I knew him first – Anne-Marie was a teacher. I used to be a teacher, so we were able to relax and chat about that and all sorts of things. With his unmistakeable facial features, it was easy to do a cartoon where he's standing in full Napoleon uniform with a foot on the car saying 'Little Napper goes to war'. He had the cartoon in his toilet at home for a long time!

When we got to the second race in Brazil, there was a big blackboard in each garage. Egged on by [Paddy] McNally [of Marlboro], I drew this huge cartoon. Alain had been playing tennis with Wattie and I had them holding their racquets with the caption saying, 'Now I'll show you how to play tennis, John, that's easy as well.' Poor Wattie. Alain said, 'You are not fair to John.'

When Alain had the second accident in South Africa, I only got to him after Wattie had brought him back from the hospital to the Kyalami Ranch [hotel]. There were already signs that Alain was losing confidence in the car. It would get worse as the year went on.

Fortunately for Prost, a gap in the calendar meant he only missed a race at Long Beach before returning to the cockpit for the Belgian Grand Prix on 4 May. His race near the back of the field was cut short by broken transmission, but at least he lasted 29 laps – at Monaco, he would get no further than the first corner. A misjudgement by Derek Daly when braking for Sainte Devote would launch the Irishman off the back of Bruno Giacomelli's Alfa Romeo. As Daly's Tyrrell began its crazy flight, it plucked the rear wing off Prost's car as it passed overhead before landing on the Tyrrell of Daly's team-mate, Jean-Pierre Jarier. The race was stopped – unusual for the time but an indication of the chaos – and Alain returned to the pits on foot.

A terrifying moment at the first corner of the Monaco Grand Prix as Derek Daly's Tyrrell flies over the top of Prost (8) and hits Daly's team-mate, Jean-Pierre Jarier. No one was hurt. The Alfa Romeo of Patrick Depailler (22) in fifth place heads for the apex of St Devote, followed by Nelson Piquet's Brabham. The Ferrari of Gilles Villeneuve (2) prepares to give the colliding Tyrrells a wide berth. Bruno Giacomelli, his Alfa Romeo minus a rear wing and wheel, follows.

A poor first lap after starting from seventh on the grid, and one of the few drivers to stop for fresh tyres, Prost made a strong recovery at Brands Hatch to finish sixth in the British Grand Prix.

Tony Jardine

It was actually a big surprise for us when Alain came back to the pits. We didn't have monitors in those days, so we didn't know what had happened. If Alain had driven the car round to the pits, we could have put a rear wing on it and sent him out for the re-start. But you could see he was quite shocked by the whole thing as you would be when a car – full of fuel, don't forget – comes flying overhead. We really needed a result in Monaco because Wattie hadn't qualified. Prost had qualified on the fifth row – which was pretty good for that car – and I remember him telling us once again to go easy on John. Not that the lads paid much attention to that, particularly after poor Wattie dropped the moped he was riding to the paddock!

As the scene shifted to Madrid's Jarama, Alain was introduced to the sharp end of F1 politics. A struggle over control of F1's burgeoning finances had been simmering almost from the moment Jean-Marie Balestre became president of the governing body in 1978. Soon after, most of the teams formed the Formula One Constructors' Association (FOCA). The manufacturer teams tended to side with FISA, the governing body, while McLaren, being an independent racing team as opposed to the racing department of a manufacturer such as Ferrari and Renault, were firmly in the FOCA camp.

First practice was brought to a halt after 30 minutes by a red flag waved not for safety reasons but because the organisation of the race had changed hands. Prost finally got going – and probably wished he hadn't. McLaren had added a revised front suspension to the M29C, Alain venturing onto the track with the modified car for the first time on Saturday morning. Coming through Esses de Bugatti, a fast downhill section, the left-front suspension collapsed as Prost braked from a tight left-hander at the bottom. The car rode over its front wheel and vaulted the first layer of catch fencing before ploughing through three more rows and smashing into the barrier. It actually could have been much worse.

Alain Prost

Several drivers, particularly I remember Jacques Laffite, had insisted a run-off area should be added at that very point otherwise I would have gone straight into the barrier. We had nothing then like there is now with Charlie [Whiting] and the circuit safety checks beforehand. In 1980, it was up to the drivers to complain. Even then, the work would not always be done. Fortunately, on this occasion it had. But the accident was not good for my confidence in the car.

While that was perfectly understandable, Prost somehow managed to put it behind him and use his repaired car to qualify on the third row, splitting the Brabhams. Even allowing for the absence of Ferrari, Renault and Alfa Romeo (for political reasons), this was a remarkable victory of mind over matter. Watson, meanwhile, was three rows further back, neither his state of mind nor persistent understeer helped by someone fitting the wrong front shock absorbers. In the end, it would all come to nothing. Prost retired with engine failure after five laps and Watson crashed into a backmarker.

It was a wasted opportunity in every sense. The field had been diminished so badly that Patrick Gaillard, the other party in the Watson collision, limped back to the pits, had a new rear wing fitted to his Ensign-Cosworth and still managed to finish sixth and last – only for all points scored to be wiped from the board when the race was declared 'illegal' by FISA.

The remaining Grands Prix would count. Alain finished sixth in Britain and in Holland. Between these two races, on 1 August, he married Anne-Marie. It would turn out to be a day of joy and sadness when news came through that Patrick Depailler had been killed while testing his Alfa Romeo at Hockenheim. The Frenchman left the road at the very fast Ostkurve, pre-chicane. The anguish and frustration over a suspected suspension failure was made much worse by the news that catch fencing, due to be installed in the run-off area for the forthcoming German Grand Prix, was actually rolled up and lying behind the very crash barrier the likeable Depailler hit with fatal force.

Alain Prost *This was the first time I had to come to terms with the loss of a driver I knew. I can't say Patrick had been a close friend because I didn't really know him that well. But he had been the first among the drivers to come up to me and offer a helping hand when I arrived in F1. I don't know why he did that but I appreciated it. He was certainly very well liked by everyone.*

The Dutch Grand Prix marked the introduction of a completely new car, the McLaren M30. Significantly, this was entrusted to Prost while, coincidentally, Watson suddenly made progress with the M29C and qualified ninth. Prost, bedevilled by engine failures and teething problems, started 18th and gradually worked his way up the field, helped on lap 19 when Watson lost a certain points finish with an engine vibration caused by a blown spark box. Such were the many and varied technical problems blighting McLaren at the time. Unfortunately for Prost, suspension failures would continue to be among them.

Prost gave the McLaren M30 its debut at Zandvoort, scoring one point for sixth place.

Teddy Mayer, characteristically with one foot on a wheel, discusses tyres with a
Goodyear engineer while Prost sits patiently in his M30.

One such failure came in Montreal. Until that moment on lap 38 (of the 70-lap race), Prost could possibly have been on course for a podium finish. The worst failure would occur two weeks later during practice at Watkins Glen when the M30 was deposited with some force into the pale-blue crash barrier. It was the last race of the season and the final straw for Alain.

Alain Prost

The mechanical failures, particularly suspension, were the worst point of the season. People remember the ones during the Grands Prix weekends but there were also some bad ones in private testing. I finished two or three times in hospital.

I remember particularly a crash during a test at Donington and there was the one in Canada, although that was probably because I'd banged wheels with Riccardo Patrese. It was a pity that happened because this was maybe my best race of 1980; I was really flying.

But the worst failure was the last one in Watkins Glen. I spent two weeks in bed; I could not stand up properly because my head hit the steering wheel. In the end, that was enough. I lost confidence – but that is the only bad point about my first season.

John Watson

Prost had his suspension failure in the penultimate corner at Watkins Glen and hit the barrier very heavily. When I asked how Alain was, I discovered that no one in the team had bothered to go and see him. I did what I thought was the right thing, what any decent person would do and went to the medical centre. And there's the little fella lying out on a table, obviously a bit battered and beaten.

Alain had become a friend as well as a team-mate. It was a difficult year for me in the team. I blamed McLaren for that, not Alain. I liked the guy; we had fun together. He was clearly a future World Champion but that didn't interfere or have any bearing on our personal friendship or relationship. That's why I had no hesitation in going to see him in the medical centre.

The first thing he said was, 'John, I tell you now, I will never drive a McLaren Formula 1 car again. You'll be the No 1 driver in 1981, but I'm gone, I'm out.' He'd made his mind up and it was clearly going to be a matter of negotiation with Marlboro to enable him to get a release from his contract for '81. If the driver doesn't want to drive, there's no point in trying to continue the relationship. You have to work out a commercial solution.

John Hogan

The car may have been deficient but you could see Alain had something. The other teams, and Renault in particular, were sniffing around big time. By the middle of that season he'd mentally switched out of McLaren and I knew it would be difficult to hold on to him. The only thing Marlboro had in our favour was the on-going negotiations with Ron [Dennis] over taking control of McLaren.

Dennis had made his mark with Project Four Racing, a small team running cars in F2, F3 and BMW M1 sports cars in the so-called Procar support races at Grands Prix. Having established a sponsorship link with Marlboro and earned a reputation for immaculate preparation and presentation, it wasn't difficult to imagine the possible F1 link, particularly when Dennis appeared in the McLaren garage in Montreal and Watkins Glen. He brought with him John Barnard, another Englishman with a blossoming reputation. Barnard had designed the Chaparral 2K, winner of the Indianapolis 500 that year and he was intrigued by the clean sheet opportunity presented by Dennis to design a radical F1 car with a carbon-fibre chassis.

John Barnard

We went to Montreal and Watkins Glen and found that somebody had decided, I think it was Teddy, that they would change the front geometry on the car. They had made up some brackets and riveted them to the outside of the monocoque. Basically, the brackets were ripped off when Prost was driving. He was most disgruntled, to say the least. I remember Alain, Ron and me having breakfast in Watkins Glen and Alain more or less saying he was leaving. Of course, assuming we took over the team, Ron and I didn't want him to go; it was obvious he had a big future and I liked the way he went about every aspect of his racing. We needed him for what we had in mind for a revamped team, a carbon car and so on. But I could understand why he felt like he did. In my view, the M30 was not engineered that well. It was not light and not good.

John Hogan

Having worked with Ron on the M1 (Procar) and been in their workshops, I knew what was going on. John was upstairs in a little room drawing out the first MP4/1 [F1 car] with a carbon-fibre chassis. This was happening in parallel during 1980. We knew we had to do something about McLaren and it all began to come together at the end of the year. Prost was quite impressed with our plans, but we couldn't offer him at that point what Renault could offer him in terms of a competitive car.

John Watson

There were a lot of politics going on at this time. Marlboro were trying to force Teddy to take John Barnard and Ron Dennis into the team. Teddy was resisting and his answer was to develop the M30, which was effectively, a steroid M29. They still didn't understand the fundamentals of aerodynamics. Part of the politics was to put Alain in the M30 while I continued with the M29. When John Barnard first appeared in Canada and re-thought what we were doing with the M29, it transformed the car. I was way quicker than Alain in the M30 and, not to put too fine a point on it, The Wiener was getting pissed off about it. Meanwhile, he knew Alain was mentally on his way to Renault at that stage. So the whole thing was kicking off. And then the M30 deposits Alain into the barrier at Watkins Glen.

Tony Jardine

It reached the point in Canada where the Renault guys were circling so much that it got Teddy's attention and he wasn't happy about it. He started sending letters pointing out that Prost was contracted to McLaren. He did as much as he could. The low point for me was in Watkins Glen when Ron said he was taking over and it began to come clear that about 50 per cent of the guys were to be made redundant.

The shape of things to come at McLaren. John Watson sits between John Barnard (left) and Ron Dennis.

IN THE END, I
CHOSE RENAULT,
NOT BECAUSE IT
WAS FRENCH BUT
BECAUSE MAYBE
THIS WAS THE
FUTURE FOR ME.
ALAIN PROST

Ron Dennis

I had watched Alain's career as he moved through the ranks of the Elf-sponsored teams, finally emerging, of course, when given the opportunity to drive for McLaren. We met in Canada at the penultimate race and he was clearly committed to staying with McLaren. He was excited about everything I told him about the carbon-fibre MP4/1 and John Barnard. I convinced him that staying with McLaren was the right thing to do.

John and I then went for a meeting, I think, in New York and arrived at Watkins Glen on the Friday evening or the Saturday morning by which time Alain had had an accident and was concussed. There had been a very strong argument between Alain and Teddy Mayer, Teddy saying that he'd made a driving error and Alain saying the car had broken. Alain subsequently left the track before we got to speak to him. I think at that point, he'd decided to leave McLaren which, of course, was disappointing for John and I because he was one of the assets, as it were, of the company that we were becoming part of.

Alain Prost

This had been the first time I had worked with John Barnard and Ron and I was really undecided. Obviously I had a contract with McLaren, but Renault were pushing very hard. I had a lot of mechanical failures, I had Marlboro behind me – I didn't know what to do. It was a strange situation because I did not want to leave – I don't like doing that – but, on the other hand, it was hard for me to ignore Renault.

I was close to staying at McLaren, but only because of Ron and John [Barnard]. I had been to see them twice in their factory which, at the time, was a small place. But I could see the monocoque in carbon. On the one hand, I was impressed; on the other, I didn't know enough to judge how it would turn out even though I also knew Marlboro was behind it all. At times like this, Ron can be very impressive, in a way quite arrogant, but I liked it. I had also liked working with John Barnard and had been impressed by him. In the end, I chose Renault, not because it was French but because maybe this was the future for me.

John Hogan

Alain going to Renault and yet keeping a link with Marlboro – badges on his overalls and so on – was part of the deal for 1981 and that was quite a step for us. I must say it was a little bit against my own judgement. I thought Renault had played bad pool when they eased him out of McLaren because there was no question they had violated the contract. I was annoyed but, in the end, I finally accepted common sense and realised this bloke is the future, so we'd better hang onto him. And, three years hence, I'd find the link with Marlboro would come in very useful when reuniting Alain Prost with McLaren.

A character-building first F1 season for Prost in 1980 as he eventually decides to leave McLaren.

4. FRENCH TOAST

For a brief period at the beginning of 1981, Prost would have been forgiven for wondering if he was going to race anything in F1, never mind a Renault. The sport was riven with one of its periodic quarrels, this one an escalation of an argument that had led to the previous year's Spanish Grand Prix being run without the major manufacturers and stripped of its championship status. Prost had taken part in Spain because he was then a McLaren driver and, by association, on the side of FOCA (Formula One Constructors' Association). They were representing smaller teams, largely from the UK. By moving to Renault for 1981, Alain had effectively switched sides, whether he liked it or not.

An immediate repercussion was being forced to watch the South African Grand Prix from home. Renault were among the motor manufacturers refusing to join what was effectively a FOCA-run race operating without the consent of FISA and its president, Jean-Marie Balestre. The majority of FOCA teams were strapped for cash but the huge gamble was to pay off on 7 February when their race (with 19 cars) ran like clockwork. More importantly, it was televised.

This sent a signal in every sense to the boardrooms of the manufacturers and their sponsors. Balestre had failed to stage the Argentine Grand Prix as planned in January and yet here was FOCA not only running a race but also receiving global coverage. As luck would have it, from FOCA's point of view, the next Grand Prix was scheduled for Long Beach in California, an important marketplace not only for Renault and their associate, American Motors, but also for Ferrari and, to a lesser extent, Alfa Romeo and Talbot (Ligier). A compromise became imperative.

A series of meetings in Paris led to the Concorde Agreement which, put simply, allowed teams to keep control of the commercial side of F1 and for FISA to administer the sport. The rules were now to be made by the F1 Commission, a committee of teams, sponsors and organisers. In practice this meant that, whichever way you wished to look at it, the World Championship would finally get going just ten days later with the Toyota Grand Prix of the United States (West) on 15 March. But there would be one tricky proviso.

Goodyear, previously supplying the majority of the field, had become disillusioned with the political uncertainty and decided to withdraw from F1, leaving Michelin to fill the sizeable gap. This should have suited Renault, familiar with the French rubber and having extensively tested the full range. Yet a place for Prost on the seventh row of the grid at Long Beach indicated otherwise. With Michelin pushed to the limit to supply all 16 teams, Renault had to make do with the few sets of tyres they were given rather than throw endless combinations of constructions and compounds at their cars, as had been their wont.

Prost at least had the consolation of being three rows ahead of René Arnoux, the Renault No 1 driver – on paper, if not on the track. Such political niceties were of little consequence to Alain at this stage, particularly after getting off to a bad start by hitting a wall and removing a rear wheel during the first day's practice. It was noted that he did not hurry back to the pits, preferring to stand trackside and watch the favourite and reigning World Champion, Alan Jones, lap eight seconds faster in his Williams-Cosworth.

In the future Jones and Prost would engage in some epic contests. On this weekend, however, Prost would be reunited with his past at the first corner of the race when Andrea de Cesaris, Alain's replacement at McLaren, attacked the Renault with a revamped version of the ageing M29 Alain thought he had seen the back of. Prost would get 20 laps further at the next race in Brazil before, once again as a hapless victim, he would be eliminated by the spinning Ferrari of Didier Pironi.

As the teams moved south to Argentina, the scene of Prost's impressive F1 debut 15 months before, things could only get better. A prediction that the Renault turbo would come into its own against the Cosworth-powered Williams and Brabhams on the long straights of Autodromo Municipal de la Ciudad de Buenos Aires, Circuit No 15, was proved correct. Alain qualified on the front row alongside Nelson Piquet's pole-position Brabham and ahead of Williams' Jones and Carlos Reutemann.

Prost makes himself at home in the Renault RE20 for the first race of 1981 at Long Beach.

Arnoux shared the third row with the Brabham of Hector Rebaque, a performance that, with the greatest of respect to a Mexican with just one fifth place as a best result from 18 races in a privately-entered Lotus, had more to do with the car than the driver. Or, specifically, it had more to do with a trick development on the Brabham's suspension.

A restructuring of technical regulations – part of the compromise to unite all sides of the sport – had banned sliding skirts. These devices, running along the bottom of sidepods, had assisted the ground effect phenomenon enjoyed by users of the V8 Cosworth, rather than Ferrari with their flat-12 or Renault with a V6 encumbered with turbos, intercoolers and associated plumbing.

The rules also called for a 6-centimetre ground clearance that, for obvious reasons, could only be checked while the car was stationary. Gordon Murray, Brabham's designer (later to bring his ingenuity to McLaren), had dreamed up a hydraulic suspension system that allowed the car to sink at speed to the point where its (non-sliding) side skirts were almost in contact with the ground, thus regaining much of the ground effect advantage generated within the sidepods.

The effectiveness of this would be proved during the race when, to the horror of a passionate crowd, Rebaque breezed past local hero Reutemann as if he was standing still. Fortunately for the anxious security chiefs, the mounting ire of 80,000 race fans in searing heat was calmed when Rebaque's engine failed. His retirement prevented a Brabham one-two and allowed Reutemann back into second place, Prost moving up to third. He may have been almost a minute behind the winner, Piquet, but that did not detract from Alain's first of over a hundred F1 podium finishes. His first win would come five races later, appropriately at Dijon in France. Fittingly, in this season of continuing political unrest, it would not come without mild controversy.

Goodyear had come back to F1 at this race, thus sparking a tyre war with Michelin and the return of softer compounds aplenty. These would play a significant part in the final stage of the French Grand Prix but, first, Renault were celebrating pole – for Arnoux. With Prost qualifying 0.41 seconds behind in third, and given his superior speed in the eight races thus far, it exposed the fact that Gérard Larrousse, for reasons best known to the Renault *chef d'équipe*, had allowed Arnoux to run even more boost for a final lap on sticky tyres.

Michelin qualifying tyres in place, Prost prepares for the restart at Dijon and his first F1 victory.

The occasional absurdities evident in 1981 would continue when the start was reduced to what could best be described as a free-for-all. The lights had gone from red to green as intended, only for an electrical fault to flick them instantly back to red and, finally, to green once more. Arnoux hesitated, as did Watson sitting alongside in his McLaren, but Prost and Piquet needed no second bidding and shot forward at the merest hint of green. Mindful of collisions that had caused problems on previous first laps, Prost let a forceful Watson into second behind Piquet while, further back, all manner of place changes took place as the field sorted itself out, amazingly without major incident.

Having allowed the race to settle down, Prost relieved Watson of second place, only for life to be made difficult with the loss of fourth gear. Prost somehow managed to defend his place and relief seemed to be at hand when the heavens opened on lap 49 and the race was stopped. Crucially, this was just before three-quarter distance. The rules at the time indicated that, rather than declare the race finished, the result after a restart would be the aggregate of the two parts.

None of the first three were happy about continuing, albeit for different reasons. Piquet knew that Renault would fit soft Michelins to Prost's car and turn up the boost (refuelling was allowed as the cars waited on the grid). Watson would also receive soft Michelins for his McLaren, but the chances of a second F1 win (his first having been five years before) for the sensitive Ulsterman had been disrupted by a break in concentration and rhythm during this 45-minute delay. Prost was worried about the loss of fourth, his mechanics having been unable to attend to the gearbox during the delay.

On the warm-up lap, Prost tried to select fourth – and found it. He held his breath and tried again. Fourth was operational once more. When the lights went green, he was gone, leading the lap and keeping Watson at bay for the remaining 21. Piquet, having led comfortably until the delay, slithered backwards and was eventually classified third, Brabham being deeply unhappy about rules that, in effect, allowed Prost and Renault to gamble on qualifying tyres for the final part. This, in fact, would be a sign of Prost's uncanny ability to look after his tyres as he claimed a home win in every sense, Saint-Chamond being a couple of hours drive to the south.

It had taken Renault until July to begin to get to grips with regulations that, in truth, had made the governing body look stupid. Despite talk that FISA was trying to assist the French teams in their quest for a first championship, Renault were actually angered by the edicts from Place de la Concorde, particularly when FISA declared that the Brabham with its hydraulic suspension was legal. Or, at least, it was when measured in the pit lane.

In order to run their cars as low as possible without grinding the solid skirts and chassis on the ground, designers now had to incorporate increasingly stiff suspension as tyre walls and suspension arms took on the role of shock absorbers. The cars were infinitely more difficult and dangerous to drive; a curious anomaly given that Balestre, in his obsessive drive to ban sliding skirts (and hurt the FOCA teams) had cited safety as his honourable motive.

Renault had started with the RE20 (a modified version of the 1980 car), the all-new RE30 appearing mid-season. Having come to Dijon with just four points to his name (33 points behind championship leader Reutemann), Prost would collect another 39 in the second half of the season, starting with that win in Dijon on 5 July.

Alain confers with Bernard Dudot, the brains behind the Renault turbo V6. In the background wearing the dark jacket, Jean Ragnotti, winner of that year's Monte Carlo Rally for Renault.

Prost streaks into the lead of the German Grand Prix at Hockenheim while Arnoux makes a slow getaway and has already been overtaken by Reutemann's Williams (2).

There should have been a follow-up victory two weeks later at Silverstone. Starting from the outside of the front row (alongside the boost-assisted Arnoux), Prost had pulled out a five-second lead in as many laps and looked extremely comfortable on this fast circuit. But running the V6 turbo flat out for longer periods than ever before would take its toll on both cars, Prost retiring with burned valves on lap 17.

When Arnoux ran into similar trouble eight laps from home, Watson took the lead to score a memorable victory for himself and a landmark result for McLaren, this being the start of a long and impressive resurgence for the revamped team and their pioneering carbon-fibre chassis, the MP4.

Renault, meanwhile, were hard at work modifying the RE30 to cope with the hydraulic suspension that, thanks to Brabham and FISA, was now de rigueur. There was only one such car available in time for the Dutch Grand Prix at Zandvoort on 30 August. Prost put it to good use by taking pole (thus denying Arnoux three in a row) and leading every lap. Such a straightforward statistic, however, does not do justice to the massive battle between Prost and Jones.

Once he had dealt with Arnoux, Jones gradually closed on Prost and, more than once, got alongside under braking for Tarzan, the hairpin at the end of the long main straight. Jones never managed to get ahead as Prost cleanly but firmly edged the Williams onto the exit kerb. This went on until lap 18, when Jones saw his chance.

Exiting the corner leading onto the straight, Prost missed a gear, Jones immediately darting from behind the Renault and snatching the lead. Even better, there was a backmarker to provide the perfect slipstream to allow Jones to ease further ahead on the straight. As he pulled a 180-mph slingshot move to the right of the backmarker

into the braking area for Tarzan, Jones had every reason to believe it was 'job done'. The tough Australian's surprise can be imagined when a blur of yellow and white to his right announced the late arrival of Prost, attacking immediately and sitting it out as the pair ran side-by-side through the right-hander. At the exit, the torque of the turbo gave Prost the small advantage he needed to resume a lead he would not lose for the remaining 49 laps. Jones, never easy to impress, made a mental note: Respect.

Victory for Prost in the Italian Grand Prix would be easy by comparison and he rounded the season off with second place (to Jones) on a temporary circuit in a hotel car park in Las Vegas. The gamblers had not been drawn from their gaming tables to watch the final round of a championship won by Piquet. But for Prost, moving to Renault had proved to be a good bet, not just for 1981 but also for the future. Clearly, the package had a lot of promise, Renault-Elf finishing third in the constructors' championship, three places ahead of Prost's former employers, McLaren.

I was really happy at the end of that season. I felt I was with a top team and we had been moving forward all the time. I'd got pole positions and won three races: not bad for a second season. I'd say the win at Zandvoort was more important than the first win at Dijon because of the fight I'd had with Alan Jones. He was very tough – he used to make fantastic starts when the car was full of fuel – and he would never back off. He'd beaten me at the previous race in Germany [Hockenheim] and I think I took him completely by surprise with the move down the inside at Tarzan. René [Arnoux] had won pole position four times. Actually, I was sure I could have been on pole more times had Gérard Larrousse allowed me to use more boost. I remember being absolutely furious at Silverstone when, having done the fastest qualifying lap, I had to watch as Larrousse sent Arnoux out again with the turbo boost turned up even higher. But I won three races and Holland hadn't done my reputation any harm, that's for sure.

The period around the Dutch Grand Prix had been significant for another reason: Anne-Marie had given birth to Nicolas on 18 August. Life was good and 1982 promised a great deal. But, as Prost was becoming aware, motor racing is never that simple. He was about to take part in one of the most bizarre and, at times, tragic seasons in the history of F1.

It began with a drivers' strike. Just as FISA and FOCA were beginning to sort out their differences, the drivers took umbrage over a new clause in FISA's so-called Super Licence that effectively tied them to their respective teams. (The irony from Prost's point of view was that Renault prizing him away from McLaren had prompted Teddy Mayer, among others, to push for the introduction of a clause stating the driver was 'committed' to his team and would 'drive exclusively for them' until the end of the contract.)

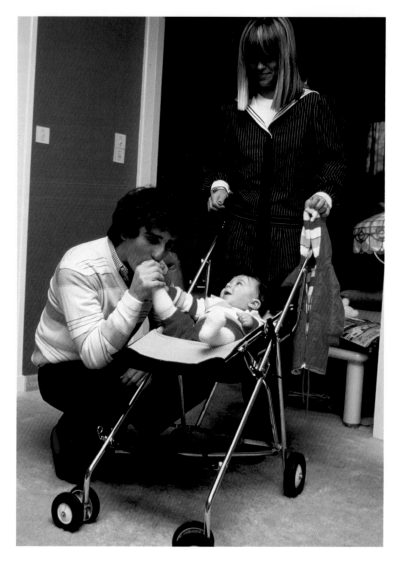

Happy days for Alain and Anne-Marie following the birth of Nicolas in August 1981.

Feeling that their freedom was being encroached – once this had been pointed out to those who had blithely signed without reading the small print – the drivers decided to unite. Rather than follow the usual course of half-hearted shambling on the starting grid which would inevitably lead to everyone racing and the matter being dropped, they knew the only course of action was to remove themselves from the pressure that would be exerted in private by team bosses.

To that end, a coach was waiting at the gate of the Kyalami circuit when the drivers arrived for what should have been the first day of practice for the South African Grand Prix. Abandoning their wives and girlfriends, the 31 drivers (with the exception of Jochen Mass, who was late) boarded the coach and set off for the Sunnyside Park Hotel in Johannesburg. As negotiations continued without conclusion, the drivers locked themselves in a function room and bedded down for the night on mattresses.

Alain Prost

It was a very unusual and unforgettable experience. Elio [de Angelis] and Gilles [Villeneuve] played the piano and I remember that [Bruno] Giacomelli gave us a lecture on terrorism and guns! If nothing else, it was unique because the drivers were completely united for the first time and away from the influence of their teams.

Telephone calls between Pironi and Jean-Marie Balestre led to an agreement of sorts and the drivers returned to the track to prepare for what should have been the second day of practice.

The lost day was not as disastrous as it could have been thanks to the top teams having completed hundreds of laps of Kyalami during limitless testing. Prost, having got under the lap record by several seconds during testing, was expected to pick up where he left off – and undoubtedly would have done had a punctured left-rear Michelin not deposited the Renault into the wall during untimed practice. The car was repaired in time for qualifying but a down-on-power engine indicated that dirt had got into the turbo. He would start from the third row, five places behind team-mate Arnoux on pole.

Turbocharged cars ruled the thin air of Kyalami at an altitude of 1,464 metres. Now there were eight on the entry, the Renaults and Ferraris having been joined by BMW-powered Brabhams and a pair of Toleman-Harts, one of which failed to qualify and the other halfway down the grid. The remainder of the turbos filled the first three rows.

Despite the uncertainty and negative publicity caused by the drivers' strike, 85,000 spectators turned up on race day, Saturday 23 January. Renault proved their engineers had not been idle during the off-season when the slow getaways previously associated with the turbo were banished as Arnoux streaked into the lead, Prost cutting through from the third row to join his team-mate on the long run towards the first corner.

Renault's yellow and white cars pulled away, Prost taking the lead when Arnoux experienced a tyre vibration on lap 14. Arnoux's problem had been caused by picking up rubber as he began to move off line as early as lap ten to overtake backmarkers (an indication of how, 30 years ago, slower cars were seen as obstacles the leaders needed to deal with as best they could rather than expect them to stand aside, as required today).

Prost was to hit tyre trouble of a different kind when he picked up a puncture one-third of the way through lap 41. By the time he reached the pits, flailing rubber from the left-rear had damaged the bodywork and left the RE30B more or less running on the rim. If he was lucky, Prost would be able to rejoin but, whatever the outcome, the chance of victory was gone. Or so it seemed.

The terrible scene at Zolder in 1982 following Gilles Villeneuve's fatal accident during qualifying for the Belgian Grand Prix.

Prost and Renault were about to defy all predictions and, in the process, introduce the concept that a pit stop for fresh tyres – then reserved for emergencies only – could be a good strategy. Prost rejoined in eighth place, a lap behind the leader, Arnoux. Within four laps, he had unlapped himself. Ten laps later, with 20 to go, he was fourth, his progress helped further by Pironi dropping back with engine trouble. With ten laps remaining, Prost was second, catching Arnoux by three seconds a lap and ready to take advantage of his team-mate's continuing struggle with tyre vibration. A win had been expected – but never under circumstances such as these. Prost and Renault had inadvertently put in motion a sea change in racing tactics.

Prost would also be declared winner of the next race in Brazil but, once again, the victory would come under unusual circumstances. He had actually crossed the line in third place behind Nelson Piquet and Keke Rosberg, only for the Brabham and Williams drivers to be excluded 29 days later by an FIA appeal tribunal. Renault and Ferrari had protested a blatant piece of rule-bending as the Cosworth teams fitted large water tanks, supposedly to assist brake cooling. The water, in fact, was no more than disposable ballast, quickly dispersed in the general direction of the brakes immediately after the start and then replaced (as allowed by the rules) after the race, but before scrutineering, thus returning the less powerful, non-turbo cars to the 580 kg minimum weight limit.

South Africa and Brazil would be the only victories claimed by Prost in 1982. As things would turn out, that would be a reasonable score in a year when no less than 11 different drivers won races. It was rapidly becoming an increasingly strange season, the majority of mainly British independent teams making a tactical and rather childish error by boycotting the San Marino Grand Prix. Prost lasted seven laps at Imola before turbo trouble brought retirement, the Ferraris finishing first and second, Pironi ahead of an outraged Gilles Villeneuve, who felt he had been duped by his team-mate.

Politics had totally dominated the season thus far but the damaging rhetoric was stopped in its tracks two weeks later at Zolder when Villeneuve was killed while trying to better Pironi's time during the closing minutes of qualifying for the Belgian Grand Prix. Neither driver had spoken to each other since Imola.

Alain Prost *I had been very close with Gilles. After Imola, he was calling me two or three times each day. I've never known anyone like this. I said, 'Gilles, stop; stop! Think about something else. You can't continue like this.' He died 100 per cent because of what happened at Imola. I was sitting behind his car in the pits at Zolder when he told [Ferrari technical director Mauro] Forghieri he wanted to do another lap, even without a fresh set of tyres. I was just 30 seconds behind when the accident happened. That was really awful.*

The loss of the talented French-Canadian swung the spotlight onto the folly of qualifying tyres and a chassis that had failed to protect its driver. But, regardless of the tragedy, the season continued its relentless programme through the summer and, as was becoming the norm, Renault led races but failed to win them through a catalogue of mechanical failures.

The one exception was, appropriately enough, their home Grand Prix at Paul Ricard on 25 July. Indeed, Renault's potential was such that team tactics could be discussed. It was suggested Arnoux should be allowed to be the lead Renault and pressure rivals on the understanding that Prost, 15 points ahead of his team-mate and 16 behind the championship leader, Pironi, should be allowed to win if they were in a one-two situation.

The thought was that Brabham would be trying to incorporate pit stops after starting on soft tyres and half a tank of fuel. Sure enough, the Brabhams led and, just as predictably, the fragile four-cylinder BMW engines failed. Arnoux then moved to the front with Prost, as planned, following. But, despite the pre-race plan, that was the way it remained until the chequered flag.

Alain Prost

Before the race, Jean Sage [team manager], Gérard Larrousse [sporting director] and Bernard Hanon [president of Renault] asked René and me to come into the motor home. They said, 'We have an idea. We know that we are not as quick as Brabham and we want to have a different strategy. We know their reliability is questionable and we need to push them. René, we give you more boost and if you are running one-two, you let Alain through. You agree?' 'Yes,' he said. 'I agree, no problem.' I hadn't asked for this but it seemed like a sensible strategy to deal with the Brabhams and, if René was happy, then so was I.

Once he moved into the lead, I stayed in second place as agreed, not forcing the pace, nursing the car – because we'd had reliability problems too. When René got the sign on his pit board '1 Alain 2 Rene', he didn't ease up. If I'd known he was going to do that, I wouldn't have let him get so far ahead. There was nothing I could do.

I was furious, not just because of the championship but also because when you give the advantage to somebody, you look stupid. But the worst part was the Renault people never told the press all the facts. All the media knew was what they had seen on the pit board – but nothing else. No one knew the true story. The overall effect this had on French people was really unbelievable.

I was driving back to Saint-Chamond. About half an hour from the racetrack there is an Elf petrol station on the motorway. It's still there – although now it's Total. Naturally, being a driver for Renault-Elf, I had an Elf card. I stopped for fuel and went in to pay. I had the card in my hand. The guy said, 'Oh, I followed the race today and it

was very good!' I said, 'No, it was not so good.' 'No,' he said, 'it was good because that little prick Prost had it coming. Why should he win the race? You really showed him, Monsieur Arnoux!' I slipped my card into my pocket and paid in cash because I didn't want him to see my name. I felt really upset.

If Prost was being put through the emotional wringer, then so was Pironi. Aside from the chilling background to Villeneuve's fatal accident, Pironi had endured the horror of having Ricardo Paletti's Osella slam into the back of his Ferrari, stalled on pole position in Montreal. The 23-year-old Italian novice died of severe chest injuries inflicted by the Osella's steering column. Pironi had driven brilliantly to win the Dutch Grand Prix and, in between and not for the first time, escaped from a massive shunt due to a mechanical failure while testing at Paul Ricard.

At Hockenheim in early August, Pironi had been almost a second faster than anyone else during the opening day of practice. He was quick, too, during the first session on Saturday morning, despite rain that made the track more forbidding than ever. Added to which, rainwater forced under a car's ground effect sidepods would emerge as a fine, atomised mist which then hung in the air. The tall trees lining the straights prevented the dispersal of the water vapour by the wind.

Running more or less flat out on the approach to the stadium, Pironi closed on Derek Daly's Williams which, in turn, was catching Prost's Renault, running on the racing line on the left. Daly moved right and executed a proper overtaking move. Seeing the Williams move off the racing line, Pironi incorrectly assumed Daly was letting the Ferrari through and rushed into the opaque wall of spray, unaware that it was being partially created by Prost's car.

The Ferrari hit the right-rear wheel of the Renault and became airborne in a manner similar to Villeneuve when he had hit a slower car at Zolder. The Ferrari landed nose-first on the track and then careered into the barrier, the nose section completely torn off. Pironi was still conscious, but in terrible pain. Prost stopped his car and was one of the first on this scene of devastation.

With Arnoux already out of camera range, Prost takes second place ahead of Pironi's Ferrari at the start of the 1982 French Grand Prix.

The failure of a small part costing less than 20 euros in the back of the Renault brought
several unnecessary retirements in 1982.

That was terrible... I won't go into the detail of Didier's awful injuries but I could see it was very serious and it's not something a racing driver needs to look at every weekend. I went straight back to the Renault motor home. Gérard said I should try to go back in the car as soon as possible. I said I understood that but I wanted ten minutes on my own. After some thought, I said, 'OK, Gérard, I will get back in the car but, from now, you cannot impose anything on me. If, at any time, I don't want to drive the car, I won't. We need to agree on that – otherwise, I stop.'

That day, in the motor home, I decided to do what I want to do, especially when it's wet. People never seemed to understand that. It made me realise how stupid it was, just for one lap or whatever. It was not a question of being afraid to race in these conditions. I like to know what I control when driving and, in these conditions, you can have no control at all.

Nineteen eighty-two was a tough year for everyone. René felt I was getting better so it was difficult for him, particularly at the beginning of the season when I could feel a little bit of tension. We had a lot of mechanical failures, all for the same reason; a small part of the injection control that cost, let's say, 20 euros. They did not want to change it because it was part of the company owned by Renault. We could have used a [more reliable] Magneti Marelli part and no one would have known; but they wouldn't do it. If we were an English team, we would have been more pragmatic and done it.

Nine times I stopped for the same reason; many times while leading the race or when one or two laps from the end. That was very difficult to accept because [Keke] Rosberg became champion with just one win.

When we had all those accidents, it became a season when I asked myself many times: 'Is this a good thing?' It's funny how you react because you're not afraid for yourself. It's more a case of asking, 'Why do we do this?' Either way, it was time to think ahead to 1983.

A more tranquil season was to follow in 1983, helped no end by the FOCA and FISA agreeing on a formula that effectively wiped out ground effect, stiff suspensions and cars that favoured the brave rather than the skilful. For 1983, F1 cars would have flat bottoms and run without skirts of any kind. The rule was introduced on 3 November 1982, leaving designers with little time before the first race in Brazil on 13 March. The fact that the FOCA teams produced totally new cars without complaint said much about an air of refreshing calm that would remain from South America all the way through to South Africa seven months later.

Another notable change over the year was the rise of turbocharging. With reluctance, the British teams had come to accept it as a necessary evil. By the end of 1983 the number of turbocharged cars on the grid would have risen from seven to 17.

The opening round of 1983 in Rio de Janeiro was a portent of things to come. Prost, starting from the front row, struggled into seventh place with a tyre vibration while Nelson Piquet and Brabham, skilfully executing a tyre change and refuelling routine, won with relative ease. Renault had made do with a heavily revised version of their 1982 car, the RE30B, while waiting for the all-new RE40, one of which appeared for the second round at Long Beach. It was of little help to Prost as he suffered a misfire all weekend in California and finished three laps down in 11th place. His only consolation was that Piquet had also retired from a race in which McLaren scored their first one-two finish in 15 years, Watson and Niki Lauda pulling off an extraordinary result after starting their MP4/1C-Cosworths from near the back of the 26-car grid.

Locking out the front of the grid in France would be a timely turnaround for Renault as Prost took pole with Arnoux's replacement, Eddie Cheever, a couple of tenths slower. The tension of racing at home would be cranked up another notch when Renault, along with Ferrari, opted to follow Brabham's now well-rehearsed pit stop routine.

Renault had Cheever's tyres changed and fuel added in 17.9 seconds, considered acceptable for a first attempt. Not so the second stop when Prost came in from a lead he had held since the start. Everything went according to plan until the turbo, set with a weak tick-over, suddenly stalled. Prost, in his haste to dab the throttle, forgot to keep his foot on the brake pedal as well, leaving the mechanic at the right-rear signalling frantically as he tried in vain to tighten the wheel nut. Prost eventually left the pit box after 24.2 seconds. Fortunately, his advantage had been sufficient to allow a return to a lead he would never lose. His first points of the season placed Alain fourth on the table, six points behind the leader, Piquet.

Three races later, Prost would be at the head of the table thanks to podium finishes at Imola and Monaco and a flawless win as F1 returned to Spa-Francorchamps for the first time since 1970 and raced on a beautifully revamped track. He would stay on top through the European summer, wins in Britain and Austria giving him a chance to put the title almost beyond reach if he won the Dutch Grand Prix on 28 August and Piquet failed to score for the third time in five races.

The story in Holland became not so much that Piquet retired, but the reason behind it: the Brabham was taken out by Prost as they disputed the lead, Alain making a rare mistake as he locked up under braking for Tarzan. He hit Piquet hard enough to damage the front wing of the RE40 and cause Prost to understeer off the track halfway round the next lap.

Alain Prost

People said I had come up too fast on Nelson, but that wasn't true. The Brabham-BMW was quicker than the Renault, particularly on the long straight leading to the first corner [Tarzan]. I knew I could come back at him in the corners but, saying that, he wouldn't be easy to overtake. I locked up and slid into him. It was a mistake but, in terms of the championship, it wasn't as crucial as everyone made out because, of course, neither of us had scored points.

Maybe, but the retirement of Piquet and Prost handed victory to Arnoux and brought the Ferrari driver into contention for the championship with three races to go. Going into the Italian Grand Prix, the incident brought extra pressure Prost didn't need. He may have led Arnoux by eight points, with Piquet a further six in arrears, but their means of arrival at Monza on race morning told a great deal about their individual mindsets. Piquet breezed in on a Moto Guzzi, Arnoux cruised in at the wheel of a Rolls-Royce and a harassed and unshaven (before it was a fashion statement) Prost arrived by helicopter, accompanied by two massive bodyguards.

A misjudgement by Prost as he locks his brakes and slides into the Brabham of
championship rival Nelson Piquet as they dispute the lead of the 1983 Dutch Grand Prix.

The problem I had with the French people had become much worse. I was with Mark McCormack's organisation and, in 1982, I had told Julian Jacobi, who was taking care of me, that I wanted to leave France. I'd had two cars burned in front of my apartment. I had messages on my answer machine, particularly on the Wednesday and Thursday before a race, saying things you can't believe.'You're going to crash. You're going to die', things like that. I said I would live in England, Italy or Spain. I was not thinking necessarily about Switzerland, which was where I ended up, but not for the tax reasons. That was not the reason at all, I simply wanted to leave my country. I hadn't been happy for a long time and you can't lead your life like that. Every time I was in the street, people were spitting on me. This was terrible – and it was only for a sport.

Just before Monza, Renault received a message saying someone wanted to do something against me. You don't know how to take it but, either way, something had to be done. I said: 'Whatever you do, it should be in a very discreet manner'. But it was not done like that: not at all.

There were three guys – very nice guys, but they had guns and they were sleeping outside my bedroom. I had never been in a situation like this before and I was laughing in the beginning. But the more you get into it, the more you become frightened. On the Saturday night, about three in the morning,

one of the big guys fell asleep in a chair outside my room – and he fell off, making a big noise! I was so afraid, because I thought something was happening.

Of course, the Italians were furious because they perceived this as an insult and this made things even more difficult for me. On the other hand, it's true that they had some messages at Renault in support. Something had to be done – but this was not the way to do it.

Circumstances would not improve in the race, Prost suffering turbo failure, his retirement made worse by Piquet and Arnoux finishing first and second. Piquet would win again at the penultimate round at Brands Hatch but Prost held onto his tenuous lead by finishing second in the Grand Prix of Europe (Arnoux having slipped from serious contention by spinning and finishing ninth). With only the South African Grand Prix remaining, Prost's two-point lead meant his first world title was by no means a done deal.

Not that you would have known it judging by the throng of French media shipped to Kyalami by Renault and Elf. Many of the journalists had never been to a Grand Prix before and it was evident that they expected to celebrate the crowning of the first French World Champion as a matter of course. Just one look at an anxious, nail-biting Prost said otherwise.

Prost is the centre of expectation as he prepares to leave the pits at Kyalami before the start of the South African Grand Prix, the final race of the 1983 season.

Alain Prost

Nelson and I actually got on very well. I spent a few days between Brands Hatch and Kyalami on his boat. Hard to believe with drivers these days but that's the way it was in 1983. Being realistic, I knew the Brabham would be quick. In fact, it had been getting more competitive as the season went on and I had been telling Renault this, but no one seemed to listen. At Zeltweg (Austrian Grand Prix, 14 August), we had a discussion and I said if we do not change the turbos, if we do not do things differently, we are going to lose the championship.

We should have won, for sure, in 1982, even in '83 because the car was good, but we had the engine with the turbos like this. There was also some question over the fuel Brabham and BMW were using and whether it was within the rules. All these things made me pretty depressed because, the way I saw it at the time, you don't get many chances to win the championship and I could see this one slipping away.

There were lots of French journalists who came to South Africa and maybe they were not going to get the result they were expecting. There is obviously pressure that comes with a championship finale, but this was not decent pressure. I remember a meeting before the race and it was like I was going to have my head cut off. I knew we were likely to lose thanks to what had gone on before.

Nelson Piquet takes his Brabham-BMW to third place in South Africa and the 1983 world title.

Prost's worst fears began to be realised when Piquet took pole and Alain was on the third row, 0.63 seconds slower than the white-and-blue Brabham. With such an advantage in hand, Brabham devised a strategy to destroy the opposition from the word go. The plan was to run light at the start – an unheard-of tactic at the time – and build a lead big enough to allow an early stop.

By the time Piquet made his pit visit without losing the lead on lap 28, the job was done. Prost was fourth and struggling with turbo lag: the prelude to retirement with a damaged turbo wheel on lap 35. The race had barely reached half-distance but the championship had run its course. Prost and Renault had failed. Piquet, cruising home third to preserve his car, had won his second world title by two points.

Alain Prost

You can imagine what it was like inside the team and with the pit full of French people. As I said, we knew the fuel used for the BMW was not correct. I could not protest this as a driver. The team could have done on the day, but they wouldn't because, they said, of corporate image. François Guiter was absolutely furious. Really furious!

For several laps, Prost had fought hard with Lauda as the former World Champion defended third place. Lauda would eventually retire – just as he had in the previous three races. It was no surprise. This was the purpose of the exercise as Lauda drove a McLaren MP4/1 with a major difference. The normally aspirated Ford-Cosworth V8 had given way to a TAG V6. McLaren had finally stepped into the turbo era and not before time, according to Lauda, who had been a driving force behind the decision to run the Porsche-inspired engine for the final four races in preparation for the coming season rather than wait until the start of 1984.

As Prost sat behind the rear wing of the red-and-white Marlboro-sponsored McLaren, little did he realise he was witnessing a demonstration of a car he would soon get to know at first-hand. And neither would he have guessed that this potentially very quick combination was being driven by the man who would become a team-mate, a very good friend – and his closest rival.

A tradition of the South African Grand Prix had been a barbecue on the day after the race. Held at the home of Francis Tucker, a driving force behind the local automobile club and the establishment of the race at Kyalami, the Sunday social provided a means of winding down for the teams while waiting for their evening flights to Europe.

Times had changed since the first F1 World Championship Grand Prix at Kyalami in the early 1960s, when the likes of Graham Hill, Jim Clark and Jack Brabham would have been only too happy to accept another example of the hospitality that helped make this race so popular. Two decades later, drivers had helicopters waiting, appointments to meet and deals to be done.

For Alain Prost, this weekend could not end quickly enough. The 1983 championship was finished but the recriminations, spoken mainly in French, were only just beginning. Although no one at Renault would blame Prost outright, the absence of a defence of their driver said as much. The three-year relationship was at an end, even if there was no official confirmation. Prost knew the score as he walked briskly from the paddock. The question was, what to do next? The beginnings of an answer would come quicker than Alain imagined when he met Ron Dennis at the helicopter pad.

Alain Prost and Ron Dennis, together officially at Kyalami as driver and team boss in April 1984 after initiating their partnership while leaving the same circuit six months before.

Ron Dennis

We were in a queue waiting for a helicopter and Alain was stood in line with us. We'd been aware that Renault were so convinced they were going to win the championship, they had bought a very large quantity of champagne. I jokingly said to Alain, 'Don't worry, there's always a positive in every negative.' When he asked what the positive was, I said, 'I've managed to buy the champagne at half price.' He did see the funny side. I then said quite simply: 'Why don't you just come back to McLaren?'

Alain was very critical of Renault in the media – because they were very critical of him. They got into a war of words and that escalated to the point where they just parted company. But Renault didn't play it very well because they ended up with the contractual obligations still intact. The amazing thing in the negotiation – and, of course, I can say this now – is that Renault paid Alain's retainer in 1984. It was quite an interesting negotiation as you can imagine. But that's how it unfolded.

Dennis was firmly focussed on 1984. McLaren had been gradually honed since he'd taken it over four years before. The four races with the TAG Turbo at the end of 1983 had been promising. Lauda was signed for another season but the second seat remained vacant for the time being as Watson held out for more favourable terms. It would turn out to be a tactical and costly error by the Ulsterman, given the sudden shift in the driver market as Prost walked away from the Renault team on that Saturday afternoon.

I HAD BEEN AWARE PROST WAS
QUICK FROM THE MOMENT HE FIRST
TURNED UP IN F1. ALL I KNEW WAS
THAT HE WAS UP AND COMING AND
HE COULD BE TROUBLE – A PERFECT
FRENCH FROG! NIKI LAUDA

Alain Prost

There had been good times and bad at Renault but, overall, my three years there were a good experience when it came to finding out what you need to do to win and, just as important, the mistakes you can make that prevent that from happening. But I knew we could not continue.

John Hogan

I didn't go to South Africa but it was only a matter of days before Alain and Ron were in my office in Lausanne. We all knew where we were going with this. At the same time, I knew Ferrari were after him – desperately. I mean desperately. Marco Piccinini [Ferrari team manager] was ringing round the world to try and find Alain Prost – who was sitting in my office. Fortunately, I had a secretary who was really aware of the whole situation. She was super-smart and kept answering the phone, saying, 'No, Mr Prost is not here, I'm sorry.' By that night, we actually had hit an agreement and she was still saying to Ferrari that she couldn't find Mr Prost. I don't think Alain ever knew – I certainly didn't tell him because it would have given him a negotiating position.

As it was, Ron and I were busy convincing him he had no negotiating position at all. It meant we actually signed him for next to nothing. He would make up for it in his second year with Marlboro McLaren but, in the first year, we basically signed him for the amount that he would have got paid for the Marlboro sticker on his helmet – which was, I think, about $75,000. In fact, Ron and I to this day are very proud of that deal – even if Prost did screw us to the wall 12 months later.

Jean-Louis Moncet

On the flight back from South Africa to France, I had talked with Johnny Rives [motor sport correspondent for L'Equipe] about Prost and our conclusion was that he had to leave Renault. There were too many problems inside the company for things to change. When we landed, Johnny – for L'Equipe – and myself – for L'Auto Journal – wrote stories saying why Prost could not stay and that he would be leaving.

The next time we saw Prost was when he was testing with McLaren at Paul Ricard. We were very happy for Alain – but he was upset and wanted to know why we had written that he was leaving Renault. When we said it was completely logical, we discovered that Ron [Dennis] had read our stories, realised this weakened Alain's bargaining power and offered him less money. Alain was not happy about this!

John Hogan

Not long after we had the discussion with Alain, I got a call from [Niki] Lauda, saying he wanted to come and have lunch. This was on a Sunday morning. I said, 'OK, but you have to come here, to Lausanne.' He flew into Geneva airport; I wouldn't even pick him up. I told him how to get to the restaurant – which he did. It was what you might call a family restaurant and he had Sunday lunch with myself, my wife and, I think, my oldest daughter. I said, 'What the hell are you doing here?' Typical Niki, he said, 'Listen, this Prost in this team. I don't trust the little guy.' When I asked why, he said, 'I tell you, he's bloody quick. Are you going to screw me?' When I said I wasn't, he asked about Ron and I said he ought to know how Ron and John [Barnard] worked. Both cars would be exactly the same because John always had this philosophy that you can't make one unique part; you've got to make a set. Niki thought about that, nodded, went back to Geneva and flew home. Ron had to do a bit of tricky negotiating with him for his retainer – but it was straightforward in the end.

Niki Lauda

I had been aware Prost was quick from the moment he first turned up in F1. I can't remember exactly when that was; it doesn't matter. All I knew was that he was up and coming and he could be trouble – a perfect French frog! Meanwhile, Wattie had been screwing around with his contract with Ron. I tried to convince Watson to do something because, as I said to him, you never know what's going to happen. Sure enough, Prost lost the championship to Piquet and so, suddenly, the best up-and-coming guy was available, Watson was out and I have a new team team-mate who was going to be bloody quick. I had done all this hard work, helping Ron build the team and doing all the development work on the TAG Turbo – don't forget, I had to push Dennis and Barnard to run the thing in the last four races of 1983. They didn't want to race it until the start of '84. So, we do all that and now this quick little French guy is coming in to take advantage of everything. I wasn't happy – but that's the way drivers are.

Alain Prost

I was happy to go back to McLaren. I knew about Ron's ambition and had seen what he and John [Barnard] were doing. Marlboro were behind them and, of course, John [Hogan] and Paddy [McNally] were part of my history. It was an easy decision to make because there was not the choice like, say, there was coming into 2015. At the end of 1983, you had Brabham and Renault, with McLaren coming up. Ferrari were not the best choice at the time. For 2015, you would have been thinking, What about McLaren and Honda? Do you join Ferrari and try to push them? Mercedes, for sure, are looking good for the next two to three years. Red Bull are still strong, Williams are coming back. So, you had plenty of opportunities.

In 1984, I was really excited about going back to McLaren. I experienced more or less the same feeling as before even though it was now a different factory. Although Teddy [Mayer] and Tyler [Alexander] were no longer there, there were many familiar faces. It was like I had left home, gone to school for a year or two somewhere and come back home. It was so much better and completely different to Renault, a team with a manufacturer behind it and a lot of politics. McLaren was not a small team but it was still a family team in many ways and I liked that.

Indy Lall

When Alain was racing in F3, I was with Project Four at the time, running Chico Serra in the British series and a couple of races in the European, including Monte Carlo. We were up for the win in Monaco but came a close second to Alain. I remember there was suspicion about his win because as the car crossed the finishing line, all his mechanics ran across the back of the car and we suspected that the jubilee clips on the air intake hosepipes were loose! We were convinced it was our win for the taking, were it not for that.

The next time we met, I was running him in the F1 team. He was very quiet, almost shy, and I don't think he has changed a great deal since then. I remember he was very likeable and we got on really well. You could sense a natural ability and the fact that he was so placid in the way he dealt with everything.

As things would turn out in the first race of 1984 in Rio de Janeiro, Lauda would be the McLaren driver who needed to remain calm. When asked to sum up the first two days in Brazil that saw Lauda qualifying sixth, two places behind Prost, the Austrian said simply, 'Car, tyres, no problem. Only problem is Prost. He's bloody quick!'

Happy to be back in a McLaren cockpit.

I TOOK IT EASY FOR THE FIRST
50 LAPS OR SO AND THEN,
KEEPING AN EYE ON THE FUEL
READOUT, SQUEEZED PAST
THE GUYS IN FRONT AND THEN
WON COMFORTABLY AFTER A
RENAULT RETIRED.
ALAIN PROST

It was clear Lauda would need to apply all of his experience to 61 laps of racing. He started immediately, taking advantage of a slow getaway by Prost and passing the Lotus-Renaults of Nigel Mansell and Elio de Angelis. On lap ten, Lauda dived down the inside of Derek Warwick's Renault with an uncharacteristically aggressive move that saw the right-rear of the McLaren thump Warwick's left-front. When Michele Alboreto's Ferrari retired with brake trouble, Lauda found himself in the lead. Prost was now fourth and about to take Mansell and Warwick in the space of ten laps. When Prost pitted from second place at the end of lap 38, the McLaren crew were horrified to see Lauda coming in behind him. The leader had no option; electrical trouble was about to end his race.

A jammed rear wheel nut cost Prost 20 seconds and the lead as Warwick seemed to be heading for his first Grand Prix victory. Ten laps from home, the Renault's left-front suspension broke – a probable legacy of the contact with Lauda. Prost cruised to a win he had not expected and Lauda did not want to see.

Alain Prost

I remember when I first drove the McLaren MP4/2 in a test at Le Castellet [Paul Ricard], I was very impressed by the power and pick-up of the TAG Turbo, particularly compared to the Renault. Porsche and Bosch had worked very hard together to jointly develop their so-called Motronic mini-computer system. This was important because each car was being limited to 220 litres. With no refuelling, of course, fuel consumption was going to be very critical.

In Brazil, I had been very cautious because I had said from the beginning that while the car seemed very competitive during testing, we had to see how it was in race conditions. So, I took it easy for the first 50 laps or so and then, keeping an eye on the fuel readout, squeezed past the guys in front and then won comfortably after a Renault retired. People were quick to notice the irony of that but I was too elated at the finish to want to say anything about Renault's problems. For me, it was a great way to start the season and my second relationship with McLaren.

Niki Lauda

In the beginning, I said, 'There's no problem. I can fight anybody.' That was my very simple approach to it. In Brazil, Prost out-qualified me – right away. By five-tenths. I thought: 'Okay; but there's always the race.' I passed him, took the lead, had everything under control and then my car failed. I drove back to the hotel, saw the last laps as I arrived and saw that Prost had won with 'my' car that I had developed all through the winter. This was the worst thing for me. I said to myself, next race, he will not out-qualify me. I will try harder; take more chances; more risks.

Prost out-qualified Lauda by an even bigger margin in South Africa but, this time, it was Prost who ran into trouble, leaving Lauda to open his winning account in 1984. The victory in Brazil might have been rather fortunate but luck had played no part in this one, particularly as Prost, forced to start from the pit lane after a last minute switch to the spare car (set up for Lauda), had carved through the field to finish second and keep Lauda on his toes.

The McLaren drivers were leading the championship but their position proved to be something of a false dawn as the next race at Zolder in Belgium turned out to be a disaster from beginning to end. Lauda got off to a bad start on the Friday when a fuel leak caused a sizeable fire. He returned to collect the T-car but had to wait for a new wing that was being used by Prost, Lauda's example being attached to the car parked out on the circuit. Hoping for an improvement on the second day, Lauda was delayed 45 minutes while a faulty coil caused problems. Then he had a pinion failure.

Prost was also struggling as he spun no less than three times thanks to the V6 cutting in and out due to a malfunction of the engine management system. Eighth on the grid for Alain and 14th for Niki summed up their problems, the race being no better when Prost retired with a broken distributor after five laps, Lauda lasting until half-distance before the water pump gave out. Such a catalogue of mayhem puts the extraordinary reliability of cars 30 years later into proper context.

Dennis's decision to run for home and find solutions rather than go straight to the next race a week later paid off when Prost qualified on the front row at Imola and led every lap – even surviving a quick spin just after half-distance. As he passed the pits while continuing in the lead, Prost had tapped the side of his helmet in self-admonishment. He need not have been so critical. A subsequent test at Dijon would reveal a faulty master cylinder that would jam without warning and then clear itself just as quickly. The offending part was binned but such an easy solution was not to be found for the piston failure that had caused Lauda's retirement.

Going into the French Grand Prix, Prost led the championship, 15 points ahead of Lauda in fifth place. It was as big as the gap would get during the subsequent 12 races even though Prost arrived for his home Grand Prix quietly confident he could extend his lead.

The McLaren MP4/2 would be suited to the fast sweeps of Dijon-Prenois but neither Prost nor his team were ready for the rash of engine failures that totally disrupted the two days of practice, leaving Alain and Niki fifth and ninth on the grid. Porsche reacted swiftly by building two revised specification TAG Turbos in time for the race. Lauda's behaved perfectly, giving him a much-needed victory. Prost might have scored his anticipated win but, in the end, he came away with seventh place and no points after two lengthy pit stops to cure damage caused, initially, by a front wheel working loose.

Alain Prost *That could have been very bad. I was lying second behind [Patrick] Tambay [in a Renault] coming downhill very fast into the banked Pouas Curve when the front-left started to judder just as we were drifting to the edge of the exit. I managed to slow down without hitting anything and just about made it back to the pits.*

It had been a rare fault caused by the screws holding the brake disc bell working loose. Now Prost and Lauda had two wins apiece, Alain just six points ahead. From here on in, the 1984 championship would be all about these two.

Given McLaren's domination, the championship would come down to wins and retirements in equal measure. Prost would win five more races to three for Lauda, but Prost would fail to score points four times to three for Lauda. And, significantly as it would turn out, one of Prost's victories would be worth half points: 4.5 instead of nine.

Winning – and losing. Prost guides his McLaren-TAG turbo through a rain-soaked Casino Square at Monaco. Because of worsening conditions, the race was stopped prematurely and half points were awarded, Prost receiving 4.5 instead of nine. He would eventually lose the championship by half a point.

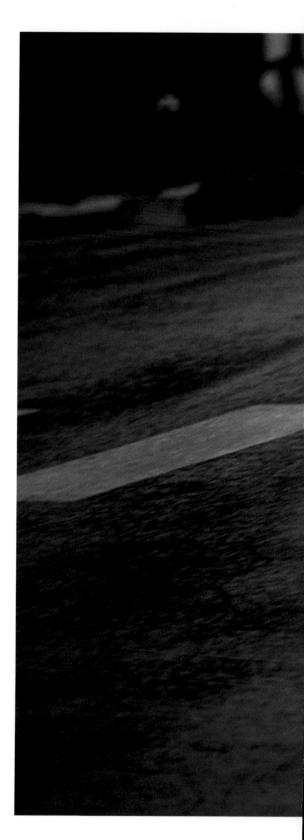

A teeming wet race at Monaco came to a premature conclusion before the three-quarter distance necessary for full points. Prost had started from pole for the first time in 1984 and led the majority of the 31 laps. He may have felt hard done by, particularly on a day when Lauda had spun into the barriers but, had Jacky Ickx, the clerk of the course, not stopped the race when he did, Prost's position at the front would have been seized by Ayrton Senna's Toleman-Hart and, not long after, by the Tyrrell-Cosworth of Stefan Bellof.

Niki Lauda

It had been very clear after four races that Prost was the fastest guy for these days with this turbo bullshit with 1200 bhp for one lap in qualifying. I had to accept that he was quicker. So, I changed my strategy. I said, 'Fine. I still want to win the championship with my car.' I concentrated on not getting upset by his qualifying speed but to work on the race, the car, the tyres; all of these things. This was the right switch at the right time because I won at Dijon and Brands Hatch – and also Austria, where he crashed because he was making mistakes, thank God.

If it was a mistake, it was an understandable one. Starting from the outside of the front row, Prost had set off in pursuit of Nelson Piquet's pole position Brabham-BMW. These two were in a league of their own, Piquet getting some respite after several laps when Prost's fourth gear began to play up. Alain had to hold the lever in place, not an easy prospect on a track known for its high-speed corners.

On lap 29, just after half distance, there was an incident that, ultimately, would have a bearing on the outcome of the championship. Elio de Angelis, holding fourth place behind Lauda, had a sudden engine failure, the Lotus-Renault spewing oil through the final corner, the downhill and very quick Rindt Kurve. The marshals were slow to react, Piquet arriving on the scene with Prost tucked beneath the Brabham's rear wing. Even with two hands on the wheel, Piquet barely managed to stay on the road. Prost, unsighted and one-handed, had no chance.

Alain Prost

Fourth gear had been slipping out several times and I was having to hold it with my right hand. In spite of that, I was able to close on Piquet and match him for speed. He saw the oil from Elio's car at the last minute. The next thing I knew, I was into the barrier. In any season when fighting for the championship, you can choose a lot of different races where you can say if something hadn't happened, it would have been easy to win this championship. Austria was one of them. I probably would have won this race because Niki came through not long after and took the lead from Nelson.

Piquet, in fact, was struggling with his rear tyres. But his troubles were nothing compared to Lauda's: several laps from the finish his gearbox almost gave up. By cleverly disguising his problem despite being short of gears, Lauda managed to maintain his lead without Piquet realising the McLaren was in difficulties. Nine points to Lauda; none to Prost.

Lauda's 4.5-point lead of the championship was cut in half when Prost won the next race at Zandvoort to give McLaren a record-breaking ninth win of the season (the previous record having been set by Lotus in 1978). If that had been a routine victory for Prost, he was to experience another of those pivotal moments in his championship campaign as the scene shifted to Monza.

Three-way conference. Prost's race engineer, Alan Jenkins, plugs into the communications box on Ron Dennis's belt as they discuss the MP4/2 with Alain.

Prost, having already jumped ahead of Nelson Piquet's
white-and-blue pole position Brabham, fends off the
Renault of Patrick Tambay (15) to take a lead he will
not lose during the European Grand Prix at the New
Nürburgring.

The scenario went like this. On the evening before the race, McLaren went through their usual even-handed routine by lining two, fresh TAG Turbo engines against the garage wall with the identification numbers hidden. One of the No 1 mechanics made his random choice and the engines were installed. The smooth routine was to be disrupted during the warm-up on Sunday morning when both race cars suffered a loss of power, fluctuating boost pressure and water leaks. Prost's had gone first, his mechanics already flat out on another engine change when Lauda ran into similar trouble.

It was suggested by Dennis and Barnard that Niki should take the spare car. Lauda, gently pushing the point, said his preference was for a fresh engine in his race car. Having won with the spare car at Imola and Hockenheim, Prost was happy to oblige, the emphasis then shifting from his race car to an engine change for Lauda.

Four laps into the Italian Grand Prix, Prost's engine blew up. The race was won by Lauda. The score, with two races remaining, was Lauda 63 points; Prost 52.5.

Steve Nichols

At the time when Ron [Dennis] was taking over and reshaping McLaren, I had put John Barnard in touch with Hercules in America to make the carbon-fibre chassis. I started with the team in October 1980. We'd done a pretty good job with the first MP4. John had taken me to four or five races as a visitor to see how it all worked. I had been Niki's race engineer in 1983 and when they signed Alain for 1984, I thought, Great! They've got the right guy back in the team again. Even though I was working as engineer on Niki's car, Alain and I always got on extremely well. We'd do a lot of work together at tests and so on. The engineering situation at that time was brilliant because we could interchange people like that. If I didn't to a test, somebody else might. So it was no problem to work with Prost.

To win the races we did with the reliability problems we had was actually quite an achievement. It took quite a bit of luck and good management. We had to try and pick a winner out of the engines that had the best oil and water consumption. They put red dye in once to try and track down the water leaks. We went out, did a run, took the engine cover off and the whole engine bay was just pink from various tiny, untraceable leaks and water migrating through the castings.

The Monza result meant McLaren went to the penultimate round with Lauda knowing that victory at the Nürburgring would give him his third title regardless of the result achieved by Prost. Alain, for his part, simply had to win to keep his title hopes alive. Which is exactly what he did. Lauda finished fourth, making it Lauda 66 points, Prost 62.5 with everything to play for in the last race.

This was the first time Estoril had staged a Grand Prix and the first in Portugal since 1960. Paint was still drying when the F1 teams had their 16th assembly of 1984, modifications to the existing track precluding pre-race testing (very much the norm in those days before countless hours spent in simulators).

When an extra day of practice was added on the Thursday, it seemed the police outnumbered the spectators. Keen to create an impression of authority, the officers, complete with batons swinging from their belts and large dogs on leashes, provided security that was unnecessary, certainly for F1 people more intent on sorting out the championship than causing a riot.

Matters would reach an absurd level on Friday when heavy rain and a flash flood tested an already inadequate drainage system to the limit and beyond. With practice suspended, mechanics began an impromptu game of soccer on the main straight. This was clearly not on the police manifesto of acceptable behaviour. Truncheons were drawn and the ball was confiscated by an officer with even more swagger than his young colleagues. Knowing about police matters (although not yet a special constable on the Isle of Man), Mansell vaulted the pit wall and demanded the ball back. An international incident was avoided when the ball was returned and an over-excited police dog bit its handler on the backside – much to the amusement of spectators who clearly had no more love for the overbearing gendarmerie than the F1 fraternity.

A delay of a more worrying kind would occur when practice resumed. Gerhard Berger, in only his fourth Grand Prix, spun and sprayed trackside stones with enough force to injure a marshal. The ATS-BMW then thumped and completely demolished the barrier, bringing another long delay. The concern was that this tremendous climax to the championship would be affected by an incident of some sort on a track that, even then, seemed absurdly narrow. With nine points for first place and six for second, to become champion for the first time Prost had to win with Lauda third or lower. Prost's chances looked better than expected when he took a place on the front row alongside Piquet's pole-position Brabham, with Lauda qualifying back in 11th place. Niki hadn't helped himself with a spin but his biggest problem had been a down-on-power TAG Turbo V6.

Lauda knew he had nothing to lose. After a cautious first lap, he methodically worked through the field; ninth on lap six, seventh on lap 18, fifth on lap 28, then fourth, then third. On lap 51, he set fastest lap. At that very moment, Mansell spun out of second place with brake trouble on the Lotus-Renault.

Prost was leading; there was no more he could do. He'd won seven races to Lauda's five; beaten the Austrian in all but one qualifying. But Niki was champion as he crossed the line, McLaren mechanics leaping onto the track.

Prost, although understandably disappointed at first, was magnanimous in his praise, a relieved and happy Lauda returning the compliment by saying with all sincerity that time was on Alain's side and he would take the title sooner rather than later.

Indy Lall

When you're working on one car – in my case, Alain's – then Estoril was pretty galling to be honest. Alain could not have done any more and that's what made it a little frustrating.

Saying that, we had a fantastic year; the camaraderie in the team was amazing. There was a lot of banter – as there always is in a happy team – but absolutely no malice. So long as one or the other of the drivers was doing well, then we were happy even if, quietly, you always want your guy to win.

Steve Nichols

It had been an interesting season. Niki had been trying his hardest; I've never seen anyone with such iron will and determination: he tried everything he could. He won the championship simply because of that determination.

At Estoril, he had a horrible qualifying and a horrible first lap – he was 11th or something. Slowly but surely, he was using the revs, the boost and the power to manage his race while looking after his tyres. Prost, in typical style, was out there winning the race, doing everything he had to do. Meanwhile Lauda was soldiering on and eventually made it to third and then to second, where he needed to be. Everyone was overjoyed except for Alain, his race engineer Alan Jenkins and his mechanics. I could really feel for them.

'Your turn next year.' Lauda, the 1984 World Champion, offers Prost a word of comfort on the podium at Estoril.

During the season, Prost had led 345 laps (978 miles) to 168 laps (463 miles) for Lauda. Significantly, looking at the average points per start in the 16 races, Lauda had scored 4.5 to 4.468 points for Prost.

Alain Prost *Looking back at '84 and my career as a whole, I have to say that was another important season when I learned a lot. It was a good year for many different reasons. I wouldn't say that we were equal within the team as drivers, but I never felt a problem with that. At the beginning, Niki was No 1 and I was No 2. And I had to accept that. Maybe in 1980, I was also No 2 but I did not feel it. 1984 was the only time in my career when I had a No 2 contract. Niki was in a better position; he could choose the testing and development. In the end I did not see a big difference. It was a fair fight between us and he won the championship*

Being totally honest, I was not disappointed. OK, of course there is a kind of disappointment when you lose a championship by half a point, but it was such a good season that you still feel a lot of satisfaction, knowing you could not have done any more. Some drivers may feel differently in this situation but if you have a good ambience, one of the best cars and you are fighting until the end of the championship, you have a very good situation. That's why I was very happy for Niki. When you have been following the great names – Lauda, Stewart, Fittipaldi – when you are young and racing in Formula Renault, I could not believe I was suddenly a team-mate with Niki. He was champion again and I was part of this history. It meant a lot. It still does. We are talking about this 30 years later and it was like it was yesterday.*

Niki Lauda *So, I did it in the end by half a point. It had been a very hard year; with Watson it would have been easier! But the relationship with Prost had been very good. He was absolutely straightforward; there was no bullshit. I cannot say anything negative about him. We had a very good working relationship, we pulled together. I accepted his performance. He liked me, I think. We never had a personal issue. He was quicker and I was running out of age, basically. He once said to me when he got his first driving licence for the road, I was already World Champion. So, Prost was the future for McLaren. No question.*

On the whole, 1984 had been a good season for Alain despite having to walk back to the pits following an engine failure at Monza. It was one of just three mechanical malfunctions in the 16-race series.

Ron Dennis

I was very fortunate in that the competitive tension between them wasn't a destructive partnership – it was very constructive. Niki and Alain were at very different points in their respective careers, and that meant there wasn't the need for them to constantly be outdoing each other.

They were both extremely professional, extremely mature. Collaborative. That made my job easier because I knew that they understood and respected each other. They knew that they were each there to get the job done. They knew that the car was a very good one. We didn't know at the start of the season that it would deliver in the way that it did, of course, but we were quietly confident that we'd approached the season and that car with the very clear intention of building something without compromise – which I think we did.

Alain and Niki derived their speed in different ways. You could see that Alain was incredibly fast, extremely ambitious. Niki was perhaps more prudent, wiser through experience and more patient – again, a product of age and experience. It meant that their races were invariably quite diverse – in fact, now, I can't remember a race in 1984 when they raced each other together. It was more common for one to win while the other failed to finish, I recall. That also added to the absence of animosity. Although they both knew they were fighting each other for the championship, it was more of a mathematical battle than a purely physical one. It was an unusual situation for the team.

It's still one of my greatest satisfactions, that 1984 season.

John Hogan

For me, it was the culmination of a real desire to get to this point. I'd resisted pulling Marlboro out of McLaren and going somewhere else but, frankly, there wasn't anywhere else to go. We were a cigarette company and I had fought tooth and nail within the company to gradually get to where I wanted to be. Which was to have a proper car, two proper drivers, Ron [Dennis], John [Barnard]; the whole bit. I was responsible for our involvement in motor sport and it had been a huge internal fight, which basically drained me, although I didn't realise it at the time.

On the Sunday night in Estoril, I went to bed. I just collapsed: total exhaustion. Winning the championship in that way with Marlboro McLaren was probably the best thing that ever happened to me. François Guiter had come up to me after the race and said, 'Zis ees all you. Well done.' On the strength of that, I had a few beers with James [Hunt] and went to bed. I only heard about the party – which was quite something, by all accounts.

I don't think Alain had ever had a drink before. He'd come through that school of non-drinking and, of course, aided and abetted by James – who was still a sort of factotum of the McLaren team and certainly at the forefront of any party – Prost got a bit pissed.

Lauda and Prost: A perfect working partnership.

FLAGS ARE FLYING, IT'S THE WHOLE NINE YARDS. AND NIKI SAYS, 'HUH, THAT POOR LITTLE F***ER.'
JOHN HOGAN

Alain Prost

The evening after Niki won the championship was, how do I say..? Memorable! I was with [Lotus driver] Elio de Angelis. It was five o'clock in the morning and we'd had quite a bit to drink. He asked me to bring him back to his hotel. I stopped in front of the hotel and he asked, 'Why don't you bring me closer to the door?' So I said, 'OK, you want to get closer?' I reversed the car. Then first gear, there was a big glass door, I went through – and down into the lobby. I said, 'OK, now ask for the key to your room.' I had to go back to my hotel in a taxi because the car was stuck there, in the lobby. Marlboro was very, very nice because they took care of the damage.

Ron Dennis

As is often the case, drivers don't drink. Alain, Niki and I decided that the music in the club we were in was appalling. We took control of the discotheque and the efforts of Niki and Alain to find appropriate music are equally appalling. This was after we had managed to navigate two cars down the very impressive steps that led to the discotheque. The two cars were subsequently parked at the bottom of the steps at 45 degrees. It had been easy getting them there but I don't think it was so easy for whoever had to get them out.

John Hogan

During the race weekend, Jean-Marie Balestre had Ron, me and others connected with McLaren come to his office at the circuit. Bear in mind, this is before the race and the president of FISA is already talking about France now having a World Champion. We said, 'Hang on; we don't know that yet.' But he wasn't listening and went on to say he had arranged a parade along the Champs-Élysées in Paris. He was doing his Napoleon bit, as if talking about the return from foreign wars.

*So we have the race, Prost doesn't become World Champion – but that doesn't deter Balestre; he's capable of anything. The parade goes ahead on the Monday after the race. I'm in the car with Niki. He's the World Champion – but Prost is in the leading car. Flags are flying, it's the whole nine yards. And Niki says, 'Huh, that poor little f***er. He outdrove me at every race – but I won the championship. He's got a little bit to learn yet – but he'll be champion next year.'*

6. WIN/WIN

As often happens when a team dominates one season, everyone else senses the underlying wish to see them beaten in the next. Not just beaten, but hammered into the ground; given a metaphorical kicking.

That was the feeling when F1 assembled in Rio de Janeiro at the beginning of April in 1985. Typically, McLaren's build programme for MP4/2B – a development of the 1984 car – had been extended as late as possible into the off-season. Testing, if you could call it that, had been limited to a few laps at Brands Hatch before three chassis were shipped to Brazil. No one had a clue how Alain Prost and Niki Lauda would fare.

Hopes that McLaren's monopoly might be at an end were raised when Michele Alboreto claimed pole at Jacarepaguá with Keke Rosberg's Williams-Honda joining the Ferrari on the front row. Behind them sat the black-and-gold JPS Lotus team of Ayrton Senna and Elio de Angelis. Prost was fifth fastest; Lauda ninth.

Alain Prost *I had been exhausted at the end of 1984; it had been a really tough season and I needed to get away to relax. After a few weeks with my family in the sun, I was straight into a promotional trip with Niki for Marlboro. This took us all over the place and I have to say it was a lot of fun being with Niki; we got on really well.*

We obviously talked a lot about the coming season and I remember the feeling was that the opposition were likely to catch up and it might not be so easy. The period before the first race didn't help because all I had was about ten laps in the wet at Brands Hatch. The next time I drove the car was during practice in Brazil but I went there really not knowing what it would be like. John [Barnard] had made a lot of modifications and redesigned the rear suspension.

After a few laps, I knew the car was good – certainly for the fast bends at Jacarepaguá. But when it came to qualifying, we began to realise that Renault and Honda had been working hard on their engines, although Porsche had been thinking more about the race rather than qualifying. I wasn't sure about this, particularly when I was on the third row of the grid.

The novelty of seeing something other than a red-and-white McLaren at the front of the field would last for 18 laps as Rosberg and Alboreto took turns at leading. Then Prost, having jumped to third on the first lap, moved to the front and stayed there for the duration, setting fastest lap for good measure.

The only sliver of hope for McLaren's nay-sayers was Lauda's retirement when the electronics black box played up after one-third distance. But, by then, he had already got as far as third place and was about to take second. That was to be a more accurate indicator of what was to come in the remaining 15 races.

McLaren's reliability, in fact, was to be better than ever. But only on one car. Starting in Rio, Prost would have a run of 14 races without a mechanical failure while Lauda would experience more than his fair share of problems. Prost would spin off in atrocious conditions in Portugal (a race marking Senna's first Grand Prix win) but he would go on to win five races in total even though the television cameras showed him take the chequered flag on six occasions. The anomaly occurred at the third round at Imola. At that stage in the season, Prost was beginning to wonder if he would ever win the title.

Alain Prost

Imola was all about hard acceleration and braking. With the car's fuel capacity limited to 220 litres, you had to play around with the computer in order to deal with the high fuel consumption. It was a matter of remembering to be patient, which I had to be as Senna went off into the lead and I was third behind Alboreto [due to retire at half-distance]. With a few laps to go, [Stefan] Johansson came by to take second. I stuck to my plan and watched the readout. It seemed to be working when, with three laps to go, I saw Senna parked and, not long after that, I came across Stefan's Ferrari,

which had also run out of fuel. I won the race. Or so I thought.

It had been one of my best races because I had to make everything perfect and look after fuel consumption and the brakes. The car was good, everything was working as it should but when I saw Senna and Johansson going away, I remember wondering how they were doing that. I soon had the answer and it was a good feeling to go to the podium after all that hard work and concentration.

We were drinking champagne not long afterwards when the news came that I was disqualified because the car was two kilos under weight. In fact, I had made a very small mistake on the computer and had no fuel to complete the slowing-down lap. Had I been able to do that and pick up rubber [debris on the tyres], the car would have gained two kilos, easy. That would have made the difference.

I started thinking about championships I could have won the previous years, particularly '84 and losing by half a point. And now, in 1985, nine points had been lost after winning. That was really hard to take. I did not think too much about the race itself but all the pressure came back when the media – especially the Italian media – were saying, 'He'll never win the championship… never, never.' In a way, it's understandable. But it's easy for them to say and you know there is more to it than that. On the other hand, when you have a really bad result and people say these things, you do begin to wonder if this is going to be another year when you lose the championship. All I knew was that I needed to get another win pretty quickly.

With de Angelis declared the winner at Imola, the Italian was leading the championship. Prost was seven points behind in fourth place. The gap narrowed thanks to what appeared an unobtrusive win for Alain in Monaco. The result sheet shows he beat Alboreto by seven seconds as the Ferrari came back at the McLaren after losing the lead with a puncture. But the more telling statistic is that Alain won by only a couple of kilograms at the post-race weigh-in. Given the disaster two weeks before in Italy, that appears to be a cavalier approach. In fact, it was the result of high consumption caused by a sticking wastegate on one bank of the TAG V6 engine. Despite Prost's previous misgivings, luck was on his side at this race. But he was unwilling to count on it for long in a season governed as much by fuel consumption as driver competence.

He was reminded of that all the way through 70 laps of Circuit Gilles Villeneuve, another track with hard acceleration and a thirst for fuel. While the Ferraris of Alboreto and Johansson won the Canadian Grand Prix driving as they pleased, Prost ran his race with one eye on the digital consumption readout. On the last lap, he intended to turn up the boost and surprise Johansson but that plan was foiled when the brake-troubled Ligier-Renault of Andrea de Cesaris lurched into Alain's path. Third place was better than nothing and more than he expected a week later when the F1 circus moved south to Detroit.

Prost with a TAG-Porsche engineer (left) and his championship rival Michele Alboreto while 'laying hands' on FISA President Jean-Marie Balestre (right).

Prost's dislike of the bumpy street circuit was intensified during practice when he tagged a wall, causing enough pain in his right wrist to make driving difficult. Another collision with the concrete when running midfield brought early retirement in a race won by Rosberg, third place having eased Alboreto nine points ahead on the table. Once again, Prost was in urgent need of a win.

It came, not where he had hoped on home territory at Paul Ricard, but a fortnight later at Silverstone, after another afternoon spent playing fuel consumption against performance on a track with a lap average of 160 mph. The championship gap to Alboreto continued to see-saw when the Ferrari won at Hockenheim, the pair drawing level after Prost scored maximum points in Austria.

Having finished fourth and fifth in two races and retired everywhere else, Lauda was 45 points behind in 12th place. The Austrian had chosen his home race to announce the intention to retire at the end of the season. But the reigning champion was to have one substantial last shout at the next race in Holland – even though no one saw it coming – in a season that looked like going from bad to worse for Lauda as he qualified tenth at Zandvoort, seven places behind Prost.

Niki Lauda

It was Prost's year, no question. We get to Zandvoort and a funny thing happened. I was nowhere on the grid and, because I had already decided to retire, all I wanted to do was finish the season off. Herbert Volker, a journalist who had written a book with me, leans into the cockpit and says, 'You're going to win today.' I said to him, 'Are you completely mad? I hope my engine blows up after one lap and I can go home. I'm not interested.' When he looked at me, I could see in his eyes that he was wondering why a guy he thought he knew pretty well could say such a stupid thing. But that was my feeling. I was the just the second driver – Prost was leading the championship. I really didn't care.

The race starts, Piquet [on pole] screws up and stalls. Somebody else has a bad start and suddenly I'm fifth at the end of the first lap. I say to myself, 'Shit! I was thinking how stupid Volker was and now I'm thinking I'll give it a go.'

Lauda was up to third when Prost took the lead as Rosberg's Williams retired with engine trouble. The race had just reached one-third distance when Lauda made an early pit stop and dropped to eighth. The gamble appeared not to pay off as Lauda was in immediate handling problems.

Despite his best efforts at Zandvoort, Prost could not find a way past his team-mate.

WHEN HE LOOKED AT ME, I COULD SEE IN HIS EYES THAT HE WAS WONDERING WHY A GUY HE THOUGHT HE KNEW PRETTY WELL COULD SAY SUCH A STUPID THING.
NIKI LAUDA

After the tyre stop, I had oversteer like you wouldn't believe and I was sure something had happened during my pit stop. I later discovered Ron had decided to put on a hard left-rear. It was his decision, not mine – or anyone else's. I was really struggling with the car but I knew Alain had yet to stop and something had happened either to make sure he won or because they thought I didn't care about winning. I remember thinking, 'No way is Prost is going to win this f***ing race!'

Lauda was to be inadvertently assisted when Prost came in just before half-distance. The stop would take 18 seconds because of a jammed wheel nut, Prost rejoining in third with Lauda now in the lead. It took Prost 12 laps to catch and pass Senna's Lotus. Lauda was seven seconds in front. And determined to stay there.

Prost finally caught his team-mate and the two spent the final ten laps in as clean a fight as you could wish to see – even if Ron Dennis didn't quite view it that way. The reigning champion kept victory away from the pretender to the crown.

There were no ill-feelings after Niki had denied Alain victory in the Dutch Grand Prix. It would be Lauda's last win.

Alain Prost *We had an incredible fight. Niki kept shutting the door but I didn't really have a problem with that because I knew he had nothing to lose even though I was fighting for the championship.*

Lauda's win – his 24th and final victory – did not prevent Prost from leading the championship for the first time since Brazil. He extended his advantage over Alboreto by winning at Monza and finishing a cautious third at Spa. His drive in Belgium took self-control beyond applying caution on a streaming wet track. Prost resisted the temptation to mix it with Senna and Mansell in a McLaren that had felt perfect all weekend, as proved by pole position and fastest lap. His circumspection at Spa meant two more points were all that was needed to secure the championship at Brands Hatch, even though there were two more races after that.

One way or another, it was to be a nerve-wracking Grand Prix of Europe for Prost. Starting from the third row, the McLaren took to the grass to avoid a slow getaway by Rosberg, only for the Williams-Honda to suddenly find grip and shoot forward, leaving Prost at the mercy of those behind as he slithered down to 14th place. He would briefly make sixth place (worth one point) only to be demoted by the Ligier of his old mate Jacques Laffite.

Patience was always a Prost virtue and he needed it as the points remained out of reach until, with 23 laps to go, he was sixth again, then fifth and soon into fourth as others ahead ran into trouble. Prost was close to being lapped as Mansell headed towards his first Grand Prix win but that did not matter in the slightest as McLaren No 2 crossed the line at the end of 75 laps. The race had only taken 93 minutes but it had seemed twice as long for the new World Champion.

Alain Prost

It had been a really difficult race for me. I was furious with myself after such a bad start but, then again, I had been lucky that no one had hit me as I got back onto the circuit. And one of the many drivers to pass me was Alboreto, who had been even further back on the grid than me. It did nothing for my nerves, particularly when my car was not handling well and I was getting involved in other people's battles. Then Jacques passed me. He had come over on the grid to wish me luck but, of course, he had his own race to run and there was nothing I could do about that. The only consolation was seeing Alboreto's Ferrari blow up – but I still needed the two points.

What I didn't want was to have to wait for the final two races [in South Africa and Australia] to settle this because that's when self-doubt can start to take over. When I made my pit stop, Ron put on the softest tyre we had and the car suddenly felt a lot better. When a couple of guys ahead retired, I was where I needed to be. I remember the huge feeling of relief as I came out of the last corner [Clearways] for the final time.

WHEN I MADE MY PIT STOP, RON PUT ON THE SOFTEST TYRE WE HAD AND THE CAR SUDDENLY FELT A LOT BETTER.
ALAIN PROST

Prost (2) makes a disastrous start at Brands Hatch while trying to avoid the recovering Keke Rosberg in his Williams-Honda (6).

THE EXPECTATION WAS EVEN BIGGER, IF I REMEMBER CORRECTLY, THAN THE EXPECTATION OF MERCEDES WINNING THE CHAMPIONSHIPS IN 2014.
JOHN HOGAN

If Prost's gentle wave of his hand as he crossed the line belied the sense of achievement, then the celebrations to follow were muted to the point where few team members can remember them.

John Hogan

I think one of the reasons it was a bit subdued was because the cars were so dominant that year. The expectation was even bigger, if I remember correctly, than the expectation of Mercedes winning the championships in 2014. McLaren really were that dominant and when the championship finally came, it was almost as if this was the sort of thing to happen every year; now move on to the next.

Alain Prost

I remember it very well and, yes, I suppose it was quite calm – certainly compared to the crazy evening we had in Estoril the year before! We celebrated with Mansour [Ojjeh, team backer and director] and I think Ron was there but we couldn't have a big celebration because there was a race not long after, so it wasn't practical. We did not know if the championship would be settled at Brands Hatch so we had nothing planned and decided to celebrate properly at the end of the year. In any case, we were doing a lot of promotion work with Marlboro at the time and, on the way to Adelaide, I stopped in Rome for an audience with the Pope. That was obviously memorable and so, in its own way, was our first visit to Australia where, I remember very well, they gave me a big welcome as the new World Champion. That was a nice feeling.

Nigel Mansell, having won his first Grand Prix with Williams, congratulates Alain on his first world title. Ayrton Senna, who finished second for Lotus-Renault in the European Grand Prix, can be seen over Prost's left shoulder.

This was the first Australian Grand Prix to count for the World Championship and rarely has an entire city thrown itself behind an event with such enthusiasm and vigour. 'Adelaide Alive' was an entirely appropriate catch phrase, not only because of the continual party atmosphere but also because the circuit ran through streets a short walk from the city centre.

But if Prost's championship celebrations had been muted, then so was his final race of 1985 – certainly when compared with the antics of those around him. Senna, having qualified his Lotus-Renault on pole, became involved in a controversial incident when he squeezed a fast-starting Mansell onto the kerb when taking back the lead at the end of the first lap. The incident allowed Rosberg to move to the front, where he would stay for the majority of the race, fending off an attack by an over-enthusiastic

Senna which saw the Lotus lose part of its nose against the back of the Williams-Honda.

For two laps at around two-third distance, Lauda had led the race but a fairytale ending to his final Grand Prix was to be denied by front brake trouble that sent the McLaren gently into the wall. Prost had long since retired with engine trouble but only one Ferrari in the points (fifth place for Johansson) meant the Constructors' Championship went to McLaren. Tying up loose ends nicely, Rosberg would win his final race for Williams before preparing to move to McLaren for 1986. Prost, meanwhile, continued to enjoy the accolades and the atmosphere of Adelaide before the long flight home the following day. Little did he realise that Adelaide would mean even more to him on his return 12 months later.

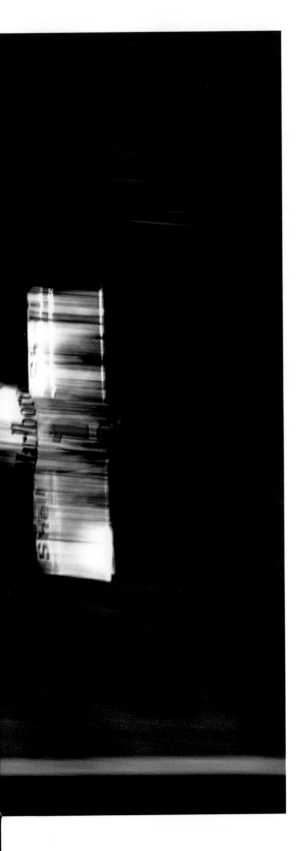

With victories in the final three races of 1985, it was clear Williams-Honda would be strong from the moment the new season kicked off in Rio de Janeiro. Not even a life-threatening road accident for Frank Williams on 6 March 1986 would cause the British team to break stride as Nelson Piquet won in Brazil 17 days later. With Ayrton Senna finishing second (after starting from pole), the Brazilian and his Lotus-Renault looked like making another combination capable of preventing Prost from becoming the first driver to win back-to-back titles since Jack Brabham in 1959–60.

Prost had more immediate concerns in Rio when both McLarens suffered engine failure, Alain stopping after 30 laps – 24 laps more than new team mate Keke Rosberg managed. All in all, this had been an unhappy start for Rosberg, who had got off on the wrong foot with John Barnard by crashing his brand new McLaren on the second lap of the first test at Rio.

Keke Rosberg

The car got away from me on a bump I'd taken without any problem in the Williams. The McLaren was just so different to anything else I had been used to. I put the McLaren in the fence and, from that moment, [John] Barnard more or less wrote me off. I was struggling with massive understeer and nobody seemed able to do anything about it. I don't think Barnard was interested. I was the new boy and the car seemed to be OK because Prost was winning races with it.

It was true that Prost had no such problems with the MP4/2C (a further refined version of the 1984 car) as he finished third in Spain and went on to almost have a repeat of the result 12 months before in the San Marino Grand Prix. The McLaren once again staggered across the line with a dry fuel tank but, this time, the official weigh-in did not rob Prost of nine points after the champagne had been opened. He then moved to the top of the championship thanks to an imperious drive from pole at Monaco, Rosberg rounding off McLaren's weekend with a forceful charge from the midfield to second place.

An imperious drive from pole brought Prost victory at Monaco in 1986.

Senna joined the McLaren drivers in the royal box, a result that kept him in touch with Prost at the head of the championship. It was more or less a single-handed fight by the Lotus driver since his team-mate was continuing to learn the F1 ropes. Senna had caused outrage at the start of the season by vetoing the choice of Derek Warwick as the second driver. Senna argued that Lotus would find difficulty preparing two competitive cars and they should concentrate solely on him. It was a self-centred attitude McLaren would soon get to know. In the meantime, the F3 champion, Johnny Dumfries, had been drafted in as Senna's compliant team-mate.

Elio de Angelis, seeing the pro-Senna writing on the wall at Lotus, had chosen to move to Brabham. The Italian's timing was not good as this change coincided with arguably the least competitive car to emerge from the pen of Gordon Murray. The low-line BT55, with the four-cylinder BMW engine laid on its side, was hampered from the start by a catalogue of problems. Monaco was a case in point. An engine misfire relegated de Angelis to the back of the grid where he struggled for 31 laps until the engine gave up. This had been his 108th Grand Prix start. It would also be his last.

Four days later, de Angelis took part in an F1 test session at Paul Ricard. Going through La Verrière, a 180-mph left-right flick after the pits, the rear wing failed, sending the Brabham into a series of cartwheels and over the barrier on the right-hand side of the track. The car landed upside down and began to catch fire. The chassis withstood the impact, de Angelis's injuries were limited to a broken collarbone and light burns on his back. But he was trapped in the cockpit.

Alan Jones and Prost were first on the scene, their sense of helplessness and frustration intensified by the absence of marshals. When one finally arrived, his t-shirt and shorts proved as inadequate an outfit as the single fire extinguisher was in dealing with the blaze. According to Jones, the extinguisher actually contributed to the shortage of oxygen when the fumes went into the cockpit. After another interminable delay once de Angelis had been extracted from the car, a helicopter arrived to take him to hospital in Marseilles. He died the following day.

Alain Prost

Elio and I had been very close ever since starting together in go-karts. He was a true gentleman; a classy guy. I'll never forget him playing classical music on the piano during the drivers' strike at Kyalami in 1982. What happened at Ricard that day was awful, just awful. We could see he was moving and we were trying to get his belts undone, move the car, but the fire was getting worse. You are doing everything you can think of, but…

All you can say is that something positive came from Elio's accident. I said to Ron straight away that there was no way I was going to test any more without proper safety and security. That's when we started to have a helicopter and so on at tests. With what we have in F1 today, Elio would not be dead. That's why it is such a terrible memory.

Tim Wright

I was engineering Alain's car and we were running race distances that day. We'd just sent him out on full tanks. We'd been having a slight problem with the sealing around the top of the fuel tank and we weren't sure if we had solved the problem.

Alain had done a lap or so when the next thing we saw was a huge pall of smoke in the distance, to our right. At that time we weren't able to communicate directly with Alain so we didn't know what had happened. They stopped the session and I can tell you it was a huge worry as we rushed to the scene, thinking it might be Alain. When we got there, we found Alain had stopped and was trying to help. There was momentary relief – and then the absolute horror of what was happening to poor Elio.

The loss of Elio de Angelis (right) in 1986 hit the F1
community hard, particularly his Lotus team mate,
Nigel Mansell.

It was a subdued Nigel Mansell who stood on top of the podium ten days later at Spa-Francorchamps. Nigel and Elio had been team-mates at Lotus for five seasons and his first win of 1986 could not ease Mansell's obvious distress. At that moment, the championship was far from his mind.

Nine points had brought Mansell into third place on the table, five points behind Prost and seven adrift of Senna. Prost had finished sixth and, as is often the case in motor racing, rarely had he worked so hard to achieve a single point. Starting from third on the grid, Alain had been caught in a pincer movement at the first corner, the McLaren becoming airborne and landing on its nose after locking wheels with Gerhard Berger's Benetton-BMW. Returning from a pit stop for a new nose, Prost rejoined in 23rd place and began a precise but patient climb through the field. It was not until the McLaren had been returned to the pits that the team began to appreciate just how good that drive had been on a daunting circuit such as Spa.

John Barnard *We were satisfied the car was safe when he pitted, but it certainly wasn't in A1 condition. We became fully aware of that when we later found that the first corner shunt, apart from damaging the nose and front suspension, had bent an engine mounting plate. Bending one of those plates in compression was unheard of. The car was like a banana! He had needed an eighth turn of lock in order to keep the car going in a straight line. Not only that, he never touched the [turbo] boost, even though the temptation must have been tremendous.*

People said he was lucky – but that wasn't so. He's intelligent. They called him 'The Professor' and that race proved why.

Alain Prost *In 1986, I always thought there was a chance of the championship even though the Williams-Honda was much better; much quicker. I really wanted to get this point at Spa. But I was young. Every time going into Eau Rouge, I was thinking, You don't know what can happen with the car like this. I had a car for right corners – and a different car for left corners! But I got a point. When racing and fighting for a championship, you know that sometimes you have to take risks – but, even so, this was a big risk.*

Mansell would strengthen his championship challenge by beating Prost in Canada, Senna then taking his turn a week later in Detroit. Prost made the podium on both occasions, third being a personal achievement at the latter.

Prost drove an exceptional race at Spa with a car that was less than perfect.

Alain's feelings about Detroit's angular street circuit had not been improved on the first day when he lost control exiting the final chicane and dumped the McLaren into the wall in full view of the pits. The following morning, Prost found a note stuck to the steering wheel of his MP4/2C. 'Differential, brakes, wishbone upper left, wishbone upper right, steering, suspension, gearbox, engine, heat exchanger, underbody, wings – all new. Three hours sleep.' A gentle reminder, not that it was needed, of the damage wrought by a rare mistake. The podium finish would provide consolation all round. That said, Prost and Ron Dennis had become familiar with damaged bodywork in more ways than one during that North American trip.

Tim Wright

They'd hired this place up in the mountains and decided to go there between the races in Montreal and Detroit. We had a couple of hire cars: I was with Alain and Jacques Laffite in one, Ron was driving the car behind us. Montreal has a huge number of traffic lights and trying to get out of the city on the Monday morning was quite difficult. At each set of lights, Ron would tail-end Alain's car. This happened time after time after time. Jacques is sitting beside Alain and says to him, 'Next time he does that, we're going to do something.' Next lights – bang! There's a lot of traffic about but Alain and Jacques get out, run back and start jumping on the bonnet of Ron's car before doing the same on the roof. Then they run back to our car and drive off. The motorists around us can't believe what they're seeing. This carried on and, by the time we got to our destination, the cars were really damaged.

When they eventually took them back to the hire car place, Ron got there first and said he'd had a problem because a moose had wandered onto the middle of the road and he couldn't avoid it. The guy said not to worry. Then Alain is next with an equally destroyed car. When the guy asked what had happened to him, he said when Ron hit the moose, it had come over and damaged his car. Talk about quick thinking. And the guy simply nodded and said, 'These things happen.' I mean, there was hardly an undamaged panel on either car. You've never seen anything like it.

Having Laffite along for the trip was a natural part of the friendship between the Frenchmen. It also explains why, two races later, Alain would be deeply upset by events at the British Grand Prix. Jacques had come home second in Detroit (largely thanks to retirements and accidents ahead of the Ligier) but the chances of doing the same at Brands Hatch seemed slim when his car caught fire on the first day of practice and he later collided with Rosberg. The resulting poor grid position would cost him dear on race day.

ALAIN AND JACQUES GET OUT AND START JUMPING ON THE BONNET OF RON'S CAR.
TIM WRIGHT

Journalists Jean-Louis Moncet (far left) and Johnny Rives (middle) join Prost and Anne Boisnard (McLaren's time-keeper) at the pit wall.

Thierry Boutsen started 13th, three rows ahead of Laffite. As the field accelerated towards the crest leading to Paddock Hill Bend, Boutsen lost control. The Arrows-BMW shot to the left, hit the crash barrier and rolled back into the path of several closely bunched cars as they crested the rise. Stefan Johansson, confronted by the Arrows (now dragging a long advertising banner with it), swerved to the right, forcing Laffite, running alongside the Ferrari, to do the same. The sloping grassy surface on the inside of the corner helped drag the Ligier towards three layers of Armco protecting the mouth of a tunnel running under the track. The Ligier hit the barrier head-on and took the brunt of the impact at a point where the barrier was not designed to give way. It took at least 35 minutes to stabilise Laffite and remove him from the car. Serious injuries to his legs and pelvis would bring a terrible and unplanned end to his Grand Prix career.

Alain Prost *Poor Jacques was in a very bad way. I went with him as far as the ambulance but the pain was so terrible that he blacked out. When I went to see him afterwards in the hospital he was still suffering and I remember I was trembling because I'm afraid of pain. It was upsetting to see Jacques like that. Fortunately, drivers rarely have such injuries today.*

Not that he would have articulated it in this way, but Mansell was the beneficiary of the accident. Starting from the outside of the front row (Piquet was on pole), Mansell had been surging alongside his team-mate when the left-hand driveshaft coupling broke. The subsequent 80-minute delay caused by the

Mixed fortunes as Prost heads towards third place at Brands Hatch (left) but drops from third to sixth after running out of fuel on the last lap at Hockenheim.

multiple collision meant Mansell had the opportunity to take the restart in the spare Williams-Honda. When he then won the race (making it two in a row after victory in France), Mansell moved to the top of the championship for the first time. Prost was four points behind with Senna third.

Having been humbled by Mansell at Brands Hatch, Piquet appeared to be slipping from contention. He would put that right with two successive wins, although the first – at

Hockenheim – would be helped by both McLaren drivers having to conserve fuel before running dry, Prost within sight of the flag as he slipped from third to sixth.

Despite being classified fifth, Rosberg had a reasonable weekend by his standards in 1986. He had dominated the news in the first few days by announcing his retirement and then proving it was not taking immediate effect by claiming pole.

Keke Rosberg

I hated the way F1 was going with the fuel. You just had the 195 litres for the race and the meter in the cockpit was always inaccurate. I had been at the Paul Ricard test when Elio crashed and I went to the hospital in Marseille with Elio's sister and brother. I was stunned, completely stunned by what happened. I decided to go public with my decision to retire at the German Grand Prix – which was my adopted homeland – and I have to admit Elio's death didn't make that too difficult. But then I put the car on pole, which was a good way of showing I wasn't retiring from the cockpit right there and then. It was the first time I felt I could actually drive this car. The problem was, when I talked about needing 'less understeer', the guys were thinking in terms of Prost's very fine margins. But I was talking about needing a major change because, for me, the McLaren had a massive amount of understeer. Huge!

Steve Nichols

Ron had said we wanted a charger for 1986. So, we had Rosberg – and I was his engineer. It was a very interesting time. Keke was such a great guy; a one-off. He had a unique driving style; very aggressive, which didn't really suit the car. The problem was that Barnard was not very pragmatic. His attitude was that the car was correct and the driver had to drive it correctly. It was like that until just before Hockenheim with Keke saying, 'Listen, Steve, I'm not a wanker. I can drive fast – but I can't drive this car.' Eventually, John threw up his arms and said, 'I give up. Do whatever you want.'

I had the aero boys check the wind tunnel. The front of the car wasn't so bad but I just didn't think we would be able to reduce rear downforce enough, especially for Keke. So I said to the guys: 'A gurney [flap] on the top [of the rear wing] increases downforce a little bit, so how about we put a gurney on the bottom. What would that be like?'

They tried it in the wind tunnel and it reduced downforce and was actually quite efficient. So we arrived in Hockenheim with the smallest rear wing we had and a Gurney on the bottom. John was sort of rolling his eyes and I remember Patrick Head doing a double-take as the car went down the pit lane and past Williams for the first time. We put the softest roll bar we had on the front and no bump rubber to soften that a bit. We were also running soft springs, which meant there was quite a lot of motion. It was too much for the roll bar, which became overstressed and broke. When Keke said the car was much better like this, I left the broken roll bar on the car – hanging in two pieces! With the car like that, he went out and qualified on pole.

Keke Rosberg (2) did not feel comfortable with the McLaren MP4/2C until changes were made to the car at Hockenheim.

I was leading almost to the end of that race and then the bloody fuel ran out again. I would finish just five of the 16 races that year, whereas Alain finished many more [12]. It was as though I was testing different management systems on the new TAG engine. You can deduce from that whatever you like but the one sure thing is that the changes we made for Hockenheim transformed that car.

I have to say that McLaren as a team was very professional and I got on well with Alain. I got to know the fun-loving side of him. He was great. Alain's driving style was unique. The way he entered corners, especially with the turbo cars, was completely different to anybody else except, maybe, Niki. The technique was to enter very, very deep into the corner whereas the classic racing driver brakes in a straight line. But with his feel Prost could brake right into the corner. He fed the brakes into the corner and was able to turn the car whereas I couldn't. I once made a concerted effort to drive just like him, but I couldn't. It went against everything I knew, like trying to get someone who is right-handed to write with their left.

The feeling that little had gone right for Prost since winning at Monaco three months before would be strengthened in Hungary as F1 established its first link with an eastern bloc country. A lengthy pit stop to cure a misfire saw Prost rejoin at the back of the field, his misery compounded after a couple of laps when he was involved in a collision with René Arnoux's Ligier. Retirement was not a memorable way to end Alain's hundredth Grand Prix. The only positive to come from the unfortunate collision with Arnoux was that it prompted a rapprochement in the form of a reasonably good-natured conversation afterwards, marking the first occasion they had spoken at any length since 1982.

Prost may have slipped to fourth on the championship table but there was some comfort to be had in signs that the increasingly dominant Williams team was in danger of tearing itself apart. A runaway victory by Piquet had outraged Mansell, particularly when the Englishman was lapped by a car that carried a trick tweak to the transmission that Piquet had somehow forgotten to share with his team-mate.

That said, the mood was not exactly soothing within McLaren as Barnard and Dennis were increasingly at loggerheads. Prost would win the next race in Austria with neither Williams finishing, but it would be the final act for McLaren's technical chief as Barnard left almost immediately for Ferrari.

I ONCE MADE A CONCERTED EFFORT TO DRIVE JUST LIKE ALAIN. BUT I COULDN'T.
KEKE ROSBERG

John Barnard *Of all the drivers I've worked with, in terms of feedback and following a direction you're taking a car with set-up, Alain was the master. He was a different league, he really was. I suppose in many ways the problem with me was that when we had our big success in '84, Prost was sort of leading the way in the sense that he would say something about the car, I could make a change and it would move forward. We were on the same wavelength. Watch him in a race and, with the first ten laps when he'd got a full tank of fuel, he's cruising around. By the end of the race he's in front with tyres that are ten times better than the other idiots blasting round corners and doing all sorts of things. Alain could drive a car with understeer in a way that none of the others could. Keke and I were at opposite ends of the scale and it was really difficult for me to get the car to work for him. Alain almost wanted it like that, because the front end was quite low in aerodynamic downforce. There was quite a lot of rear wheel bias aerodynamically with him. A lot of drivers want to charge up to the corner and wrench the wheel round. The car then just rolls into the outside front wheel and they start to lose the back end. I don't know whatever it was Alain did, but he never did that in the corner. He would approach the corner just that fraction easier, turn in that fraction easier but then, with the turbo engine, he'd got the throttle open long before the others. So he's out the corner with maximum traction because he's got all his aero based at the back and he's gone. Niki was not too far away from Prost's set-up but Keke just couldn't handle it.*

Alain was brilliant at looking after his tyres and telling you when a tyre was going off. You'd do a ten-lap test and he could say that this tyre is going to be too strong for the race or too soft or whatever. The race might be 60 or 70 laps and you need to know how a particular tyre will last. His ability to separate the tyre data and feel what the chassis was doing was unbelievable. I've never met anyone who could separate the two so well. I guess the problem for me was that I'd got used to Prost and none of the other drivers were like him.

Prost knew the McLaren inside out.

With four races remaining and the same number of drivers – Mansell, Piquet, Prost and Senna – in with a mathematical chance, the championship pendulum continued to swing as Mansell led Piquet to a Williams one-two in Italy. When Prost came away from Monza empty-handed, it was as if he had been tempting fate beforehand.

Tim Wright

Alain and I had a really good relationship. He used to wind me up and ask me to do things he didn't think I would carry through. At Monza, he took me to one side and said he didn't think the race car was performing properly and he'd need to take the T-car. He had qualified on the front row with the Williams drivers and Senna behind us, so you can imagine this really wound me up. He kept going on about it to the point where I was about to agree to the switch – and then he backed off. It was obviously a bit of a joke but the irony was that, when we got on the grid, the electrics failed on the race car. We couldn't get it to start. So, after everything Alain had been saying, he had no option but to start from the pit lane in the spare car. There was a bit of a fuss about making the switch too late but, in the end, it didn't matter. The engine on that car failed just after he had got himself up to fifth and into the points. He didn't try making the joke again.

If he was upset by that result, Alain's priorities would change completely the following week when Daniel, his elder brother, died of cancer.

Alain Prost

Daniel had been very ill for quite a long time. In '85, he was not in good shape, in '86 he was much worse and I always had this in mind. He started with a brain tumour, had the operation, but then he had cancer which was something different. He smoked a lot and was sick very often. Throughout my career, he had been the one fascinated by racing and passionate about it. He was really good when he raced go-karts but, unfortunately, he was always sick. The feeling grew that I was doing this because of him and, in a way, for him. I was always thinking about Daniel. He was so nice but, because you wonder if he might be jealous of what you are doing, you have very strange feelings. It was really difficult in 1986 but, because he was so bad, in some ways it was a relief in the end. There is no doubt that he gave me extra power. Going into the final three races, I was doing this for Daniel as much as for myself.

When Mansell won in Portugal and Prost inherited second place after Piquet spun off, Senna not only ran out of fuel but also championship options. Now it was between three as they headed for the penultimate round in Mexico – and it remained that way as Prost finished second, ahead of Piquet (fourth) and Mansell (fifth).

Indy Lall *Having been working in the USA and come back to McLaren halfway through 1985, I was back on Alain's car as No 1 mechanic for '86. It was very much a continuation of where we had left off. We were a really strong team. It seemed that Alain had matured in terms of how he was thinking and approaching things. He knew how the system worked but he never used it to his advantage. He was very much a team player. At the time, I knew nothing about Daniel passing away. He never mentioned it and we had no idea.*

We didn't have the fastest car but Alain was managing his races and scoring points through a mix of guile, speed and intelligence. I certainly didn't underestimate what might be possible in the final race even though we were definitely being seen as the outsiders.

There was no question that the Williams-Honda was the stronger package and, had Mansell remembered to put his car in gear on the grid, he could possibly have become World Champion in Mexico by finishing higher than fifth. In terms of championship favourite, Prost was considered by most to be the third man in Adelaide.

Predictions appeared to be on the money when Mansell took pole with Piquet alongside. Prost was fourth, more than a second away from Mansell's pace and knowing he would have to contend with the disruptive element associated with Senna starting from third. But, as Prost said, anything could happen in an 82-lap race lasting for almost two hours. Prescient words, maybe, but only a scriptwriter with a vivid imagination could come up with what was about to happen during a tense afternoon on Sunday 26 October 1986.

Mansell's points advantage was such that third place or higher would be good enough. Prost and Piquet knew they simply had to win. It was predictable, therefore, that Piquet should shoot into the lead with Mansell eventually settling into a comfortable third place. Prost held a watching brief for a couple of laps before, almost unnoticed, he eased into fourth and then took third from Mansell and second from Piquet – who then spun and fell behind Mansell.

The race was now being led by Rosberg, clearly determined to end his F1 career with a win. Then two events – both related to tyres – exerted significant influence over the outcome of this delicately poised championship.

On lap 32, Prost suffered a punctured right-front tyre but made it back to the pits. The stop took what seemed an inordinately long 17 seconds.

Indy Lall *The front jack was a standard quick-lift of the type that most teams used. The puncture meant the front of the car was low to the ground but, quite honestly, it wasn't a big issue. That's how long it took in those days in a situation like that.*

Prost may have been cursing his luck as he rejoined in fourth place but it would become the moment that saved him and, coincidentally, led Williams into a blind alley.

Nelson Piquet and Nigel Mansell join Prost on the pit wall.

From the outset, Goodyear had said they would check wear-rate as the race went on and advise teams accordingly. The tyre technicians seized the opportunity to examine Prost's discarded rubber. From what they could see, wear was not a problem. Word went out that drivers could run non-stop. Thirty-one laps later, the situation changed dramatically. But, crucially, no one realised it straight away.

Rosberg had continued to lead while, at the same time, wondering how he could assist Prost to the victory he needed. The conundrum was partially answered on lap 63 when Rosberg heard and felt what he thought was an engine failure while accelerating hard. Switching off immediately, he coasted to a halt and climbed from a F1 car for the last time.

Keke Rosberg

In your last race, the most important thing is to come out of it in one piece. Even if you've never been scared before, in your last race you can't avoid it. I had a 28-second lead.

Flat out on the straight, there was a huge bang. I thought the crankshaft had fallen off. I switched off, parked up, looked underneath. No oil? That's strange. Then I walked away. I didn't realise it was a rear tyre until a marshal told me. I could have driven to the pits on the rim, got a new tyre and maybe won my last race. It was a big disappointment but later they found both my front discs were finished. Another lap or two and I would have been in the wall anyway. I didn't feel so bad after that.

Had Rosberg examined his right-rear tyre, he would have seen the cause of the vibration and what he described as the 'grrr' sound that gave the impression of a broken crankshaft. The tyre was still inflated but the flailing rubber from a delaminating tread had signalled a serious problem, not just for Rosberg but potentially for others still running.

One lap later, Mansell suffered a spectacular left-rear failure while reaching in excess of 185 mph on Brabham Straight. With the car lurching precariously in a shower of sparks, its right-front wheel pawing the air, Mansell somehow managed to maintain a reasonably straight course and come to a safe halt in the escape road at the end of the straight. His championship was as shot to pieces as the left-rear tyre.

Piquet now led both the race and, in theory, the championship. But Williams faced a dilemma. With 20 laps to go, they could not risk another failure. Piquet was summoned for a tyre change.

Now Prost led with tyres which, of course, were comparatively fresh. If Prost stayed in front and Piquet, having rejoined second, failed to catch him, a successive title would be his.

Easier said than done. With the on-board computer telling him he was five laps on the wrong side of finishing and countless memories of the TAG Turbo running out of fuel, Prost drove as quickly as he dared knowing that Piquet was making massive inroads.

Alain crossed the line with four seconds to spare. Pulling over immediately, the 1986 F1 World Champion, not demonstrative at the best of times but driven at this moment by a surge of relief and adrenalin, climbed from the cockpit and leapt in the air.

Ron Dennis *The one thing I remember about Adelaide more than anything else is the picture of Alain beside the car just after he had stopped. This was an era where post-race scrutineering of the cars was such that it was clearly an advantage not to complete the slowing down lap. Alain parked the car after the start–finish line and then there was this picture of him jumping in the air. He was a foot or more in the air. It was an amazing picture and it still holds very clearly in the memory.*

John Hogan *I'm notorious for leaving Grands Prix as early as I can, on the simple basis that on Sunday morning, it's all done. What's going to be is going to be, so you might as well make your way home. In Adelaide, obviously, you couldn't make your way home, so I was sitting with a friend of mine on the Sunday morning, watching the warm-up as you did in those days and thinking, 'Jesus, how much are Williams going to win by?' I said to this guy, 'Let's be sensible. Let's go back to the hotel, have a nice lunch and watch it on the TV.'*

So we're back at the hotel, which was only 15 minutes or so from the track, having a few Fosters and watching the race. I could see Keke was really happy with the

Glen Dix prepares to flag home Prost at the end of a hugely dramatic race in Adelaide.

car and I was thinking he might actually win this race – which would have been good because he was a great driver and because of everything he'd been through with Barnard.

All of a sudden, Mansell's tyre goes boom! 'Shit! This changes everything. Let's get back to the track.' I was there right at the end. It was really marvellous; a wonderful victory. Coming on the back of two championships for Marlboro McLaren, this obviously was a brilliant way to end the season. They rarely come more dramatic than that.

Indy Lall I was obviously over the moon with a result like that. On a personal note, it had been a sad year for me because my father had passed away. He had been a commercial goods mechanic and he desperately didn't want his lad to go through what he'd gone through. He'd had his own garages and then lost it all. I had been spending my entire career until that point trying to convince him that this was a different kind of mechanic. I just wanted to share this moment with him but, obviously, I couldn't. But it was a moment I'll never forget. It had been a flat-out race – absolutely full-on racing – which was one of the reasons why everyone enjoyed it that much.

The guy waving the chequered flag was called Glen Dix. Wearing a brightly coloured jacket and with a slightly bowed head, he really did it with a flourish each year. He became an iconic emblem of Adelaide. I asked him if I could have the chequered flag and he was more than happy to hand it over. I was really chuffed with that.

Once we had packed up, we went back to the hotel for a fantastic party. It was not totally exclusive, but not anyone could walk in. Ron said, 'As you've won the championship, you can decide who comes in.' There was a big burly security guard on the door and the boys said to come and ask us if there was someone at the door he wasn't sure about. We could have made a fortune that night with the number of hangers-on wanting to come in. The party was brilliant because the whole team was there and, of course, Alain.

Alain Prost It had been a very hard year: Elio, Jacques and then my brother. But on the sporting side, I have to say 1986 was one of my best seasons. I knew the Williams were good but, thanks to having been with McLaren for three years and working so well as a team, I always thought we had a chance. But I didn't expect a finish like that!

I remember the last few laps. I had been so preoccupied that I hadn't been able to think about looking after the fuel. I could see the readout was showing zero but I thought there was no point in trying to back off because Nelson was coming after me. I had to go for it – and hope. You can't believe the feeling when I saw the flag and crossed the line. But perhaps the best feeling of all came the following morning. I was going down to breakfast and the morning newspapers had been left outside the bedroom doors. The headline said: PROST WINS ADELAIDE THRILLER. And there was the photo of me, jumping for joy beside the car. I'll never forget that moment. Absolutely fantastic.

8. MISH-MASH

Nelson Piquet won the 1987 World Championship while standing still. The Brazilian was in the Williams garage at Suzuka, having vacated his car momentarily during the first day of practice for the Japanese Grand Prix. Glancing at the television screen, Piquet saw Nigel Mansell dump his Williams into the barrier, injure his back and write himself out of the race and the championship.

The feeling of anti-climax surrounding Piquet's sudden acquisition of his third title summed up a rather lacklustre season as he won through the consistent accumulation of points rather than deeds of derring-do. F1 had travelled to Japan for the first time since 1977 in the hope of seeing the fight between the Williams drivers run all the way to the final race in Australia but the teams had scarcely unpacked at Suzuka when Mansell put himself in hospital.

Losing the services of Mansell in their home race was only the beginning of a bad weekend for Honda. The Englishman had started from the front row at every race thus far. Following his crash, the best Honda could manage on the grid at Suzuka was fifth – blown off by the turbos from Ferrari, TAG-Porsche and Ford. And this on a track owned by Honda.

There was worse to come in the race when Gerhard Berger's Ferrari started from pole and was never challenged. The leading Honda runners – Piquet and Ayrton Senna – spent most of the race waging a war that seemed to have Brazilian honour at its roots.

Piquet didn't just lose the fight; he retired in a cloud of ignominy as the Williams crawled into the pit lane and spewed hot, black liquid onto the immaculate white concrete. By ducking and diving in the slipstream of Senna's Lotus, Piquet had collected enough rubber and debris in the sidepods of his Williams to overheat the six-cylinder pride of Japan. Having retired just once in the previous 13 races (he also missed one through injury), Piquet had ended this one as the only member of the top six starters to fail to reach the finish.

Nelson Piquet had no need for a push-start when it came to winning the 1987 championship, particularly after his main challenger and Williams-Honda team-mate had crashed during practice for the penultimate race.

It may have been Ferrari's first win for more than a year but such a welcome result for Maranello almost certainly would have been postponed had Prost not picked up a puncture at the beginning of the second lap. Starting from the outside of the front row and fastest by some margin in the revealing race morning warm-up, Alain had been confident of victory on an abrasive track that needed careful management of tyres.

Such promising territory for the Frenchman would be trashed in every sense by two of his fellow countrymen when Philippe Alliot and René Arnoux collided at the start and created debris to be collected by Prost's left-rear Goodyear. Happening as it did at the start of a lap, the subsequent 3.6-mile crawl to the pits cost Alain two laps. It was the prelude to a stunning comeback to seventh place as he set fastest lap after fastest lap, establishing a new record 1.7 seconds quicker than Berger's best. It summed up a season that may have been scrappy by the rising standards of Prost and McLaren but one which was inevitable given the march of time in this phase of the F1 process and the McLaren's development.

Rosberg had been replaced by Stefan Johansson and the most significant technical change had been an internal regrouping following Barnard's departure. Steve Nichols stepped up to the role of F1 project leader, with Gordon Murray moving from Brabham to become technical director.

Gordon Murray

I arrived very late in 1986. The car for '87 had already been designed and, to be honest, it was a bit of a mish-mash. It was committee-designed, which is never a good thing. Meanwhile, I was discovering that I had a massive task away from the track. There was a lack of communication and back-up. My job, apart from the racing, was doing stuff such as redesigning and building the design office, establishing meeting rooms – there wasn't even a meeting room for the technical staff – and generally getting systems in place, building test rigs for gearboxes, measuring chassis and engine torsions and so on. I was amazed to find McLaren didn't have an autoclave. And so it went on. I also had to spend time getting rid of a few people and finding new recruits. Luckily for me, McLaren had some very good people manufacturing in the factory and competent engineers running the race and test teams.

TO BE HONEST, THE 1987 CAR WAS A BIT OF A MISH-MASH.
GORDON MURRAY

Stefan Johansson (right) shares the podium with Prost and Piquet in Brazil at the start of a season Johansson rates as one of his best in F1.

Steve Nichols

After John Barnard left, we'd had a meeting to decide how to remain as competitive as possible for the last few races of '86 – which, thankfully, we managed to do – and then to think about the '87 car. We had relatively little time before the new season started in Rio. Basically, there were a lot of good things about the '86 car [MP4/2C] and it was decided not to change things such as the suspension because the existing car's handling and tyre wear were good and there would be considerable work for minimal gain if we made any big changes.

The one thing we did do on the '87 car [MP4/3] was finally reshape the tank section to deal with the reduction from 220 to 195 litres, MP4/2C having been adapted to cope with that rather than the tank being built from scratch. But there could be no getting away from the fact that the TAG-Porsche was getting rather long in the tooth and the word was that this would be their last season. We didn't expect much – so the first race turned out to be a bit of a surprise.

The surprise was that Prost won. It had been a typical textbook race by the reigning champion, Prost starting from fifth on the grid, moving into third at the end of lap eight and taking the lead just before his first pit stop, moving back in front five laps later. He stayed there despite making another stop, the difference being that everyone else needed a fourth set of tyres. When he completed the 61st and final lap in the searing heat, Prost looked completely unflustered as he stepped from the car.

Neil Oatley

I joined McLaren from Williams in December 1986. I worked with Gordon on a couple of things in the new factory in Woking Business Park [Albert Drive] and then went to the old factory [Boundary Road] to help with work on the 1987 car, just drawing up bits and pieces really.

I never actually met Alain until the first practice day in Rio. I didn't do any of the winter tests and the plane out to Brazil couldn't leave because of a technical problem and we had to go home. I didn't actually arrive in Rio until midnight on the Wednesday; the first time I spoke to Alain was when plugging in the radio headset at the track the next morning.

The car was based around more or less the same chassis and running gear from '86. It wasn't really that different to what Alain had been driving for the previous three seasons. He knew the car pretty well. It was fairly straightforward to work on and set up, which meant there was a lot of in-built knowledge.

In those days, Rio was incredibly tough on tyres – which suited Alain down to the ground. He had this uncanny ability to nurse the car and tyres. For the first few laps, he didn't look that quick but, typically, he gradually came forward and won the race. He made my job seem easy.

Such an encouraging start to the season was about to be undermined at the next race by the first hint of an enduring problem. Prost had moved into second place and was about to threaten Mansell's lead of the San Marino Grand Prix when an alternator belt failed. Never having experienced this problem before, the TAG-Porsche engineers assumed it was an unfortunate one-off – particularly when Prost won the next race at Spa-Francorchamps to equal Jackie Stewart's record of 27 Grand Prix victories. Alain was leading the championship. But not for long.

Third place at Monaco would disappear along with the oil pressure on his V6 with just three laps to go. Prost did manage to finish third in Detroit but a similar result in France would not mask Alain's mounting frustration with an engine that had not run properly for most of the race.

Matters got worse at Silverstone when fourth place was lost thanks to a broken clutch bearing. It damaged a sensor that fed information to the engine control unit. Mindful of its duty, the computer duly shut down the V6 when information ceased to come through. A walk back to the pits allowed Prost time to consider the team's woeful reliability. And it was not over yet.

Sitting in the open press tribune with an uninterrupted view of the stadium at Hockenheim, journalists covering the German Grand Prix were drafting their opening paragraphs on the theme of Prost's 28th win breaking Stewart's record. With a handful of laps remaining, Alain had defeated both Williams-Hondas in a straight fight, Mansell's subsequent retirement from second place seemingly assuring Prost of this landmark victory. Then the McLaren rolled to a halt at the far end of the circuit. The alternator belt had broken yet again, another two having failed during testing.

Prost makes a cautious start before going on to lead a McLaren one-two at Spa (top left). Prost gets away from the middle of the grid in Austria (bottom left) while Johansson is about to become involved in a multi-car collision as Mansell's slow-starting Williams causes a bottleneck and Patrese's Brabham becomes airborne. A calmer race for Prost into third place in Detroit (right).

Neil Trundle

I went to a lot of the races in 1987 as travelling fabricator. I particularly remember Detroit. I don't know what prompted me to do this but I looked in the footwell and discovered that, because the circuit was incredibly bumpy, the shock absorbers were pushing through the bulkheads. Calm as you like, Gordon said, 'We'll put some big load spreaders on it and it'll be all right.' It was. Very cool; I remember being very impressed by that.

But the big problem in 87 was the belt failures involving parts costing no more than 50p. With the first failure [Imola], Honda said that maybe a stone got in. But when it kept happening, they set about redesigning the belt by making it a double-V [instead of single], which meant it had twice the width and strength. They needed that because there was a lot of tension in those belts. Once the belt had been modified, it was virtually bullet proof – but too late, because I reckon those failures cost Alain the championship.

Prost eventually finished fourth on the table, 27 points behind Piquet but with the same number of wins. Alain's third and final victory of 1987 in Portugal was the most significant for a number of reasons.

Alain Prost

Estoril was a long and really hard race and I'd made things more difficult for myself by having a bad practice and not qualifying very well. The race had to be stopped and restarted because of a shunt and then my first set of tyres were vibrating very badly for some reason. But once I'd made my stop [and others such as Senna had retired], I found myself second and some way [16 seconds] behind Gerhard [Berger], who was really pushing hard. But I gave it everything, running full boost – I had nothing to lose – and pushing the car to the limit all the way. I began to catch the Ferrari but I knew Gerhard would be very hard to overtake and the only chance I had was to force him into a mistake. I got to within a few seconds of Gerhard with three laps left – and then he spun. I must say, that was one of the hardest and best races I ever had. To beat Jackie's record made it seem even sweeter. I remember celebrating quietly that evening with Jacques Laffite and some friends. I really enjoyed the whole day.

Alain is joined on the podium in Portugal by Gerhard Berger (left) and Nelson Piquet.

Prost managed to finish third despite the McLarens being
off the pace in Hungary (above right).

Sir Jackie Stewart

I remember at the time thinking that if I was still racing in 1987 [Stewart had retired at the end of 1973], I would have modelled my approach on Alain's. He was so committed to the job that people tended to take his talent and ability for granted. The thing that put him above the rest at that time was his attitude. He was patient and mentally able to deal with whatever situation confronted him. All the great drivers have a latent talent – a God-given gift. But the thing that sets the really great ones apart is the ability to compartmentalise emotion, take it away

from everything and think calmly and clearly. Alain was able to do that and it would stand him in good stead later on when dealing with Ayrton Senna as his team-mate.

Prost's team-mate in 1987, Johansson, brought the other McLaren home fifth in Portugal. This result, coupled with a handful of podium finishes, would help place the Swede just 16 points behind Prost at the end of an eventful season for the 31-year-old.

Stefan Johannson

It had been a fantastic experience because I probably learned more in that one year than I did in my entire career before in terms of how to manage a race weekend, how to set up the car and how you analyse everything. It was a totally different method compared to what I had been used to.

Alain was unique in the way he went about the management of the car from a driver's perspective. It's something I've carried with me ever since. For the first couple of races, my brain was just fried. I was struggling to keep up. But then, when you start understanding the method, you start to appreciate it makes everything very simple, very clear and very precise.

It was not only a fantastic experience from a working perspective but from a human perspective as well. Alain and I became very good friends and enjoyed spending time together. We had a lot of fun once we switched off work and did what you do in life as human beings. For me it was a very, very positive experience all round. It was intense in the way it should be intense, but not in a way that it was distracting. It was very good and very open.

In those days, we had no data to look at and I really wish I had been with Alain at a time when there were readouts to compare because, obviously, you can learn so much. I'd love to have been able to see just where his lap time was coming from! He was bloody quick – we all know that – but it wasn't just his natural ability at the wheel; he was managing everything connected with going racing.

Alain made me realise that you need to look at it in a business sense, as if the driver is the CEO of the car. That's given me a massive amount of help in everything I've done in racing since then. It's almost like viewing every person in the team as your employee. They're all around you, working with you. Alain was an absolute master at controlling everybody – including Ron, even if Ron didn't see it that way. But there was no doubt in my mind that Alain had Ron wrapped round his finger. Absolutely.

As I said, his attitude was to look at it as a business. 'I'm the boss of this car. This is the car that's going to win the World Championship and all these people are working together to achieve that.' He could manoeuvre and manipulate them to move the thing in the direction he wanted it to go.

As a driver, as long as you deliver, I don't think anyone cares. I'd say that was my weakness in that I was too nice. I wasn't too much of a pain in the arse. But you need to be in order to get to that absolute top level. Alain could do it but without upsetting people. It was textbook stuff. I have nothing but great memories of my year with Alain and McLaren.

Gordon Murray

When I had joined McLaren and asked for the sheets covering the failures they'd had in '86 – not just the gearbox, everything – cracked wishbones, failed joints, engine problems – they said they didn't have any. They said John Barnard kept all that sort of information in his head. So, for my first year in 1987, I kept a record. We had 74 failures. The next year, we had 14 because we had systems in place by then. But, for '87, it meant the energy I had left for racing with Prost and Johansson, and sorting the guys out at the circuit, was pretty minimal. That year was a bit of a whirlwind and, on top of that, the car wasn't terribly competitive.

To make matters even worse, when Ron told Alain I was joining the team as technical director, Alain was very concerned because I had a reputation for walking around in plastic sandals and big sunglasses and biting my fingernails – and he said as much. It got back to me, so we had a little word in the beginning to get off on the right foot and he wrote me a note apologising – which I've still got somewhere. But it meant we didn't actually kick off on exactly the right foot while I was in the middle of trying to get McLaren's systems licked into shape. So, I really don't remember much about my first year, although I do recall it being fine working with Alain and also Stefan, who was also a good guy; a nice guy to have in the team. My focus was on '88, to be honest.

Neil Oatley

Alain was very different to the drivers I had been used to immediately before that. From my point of view as a new boy to the team, he was very accommodating. In those days, it was far less intense than it is now. There was no data and the whole thing was more intuitive. I don't remember '87 being a particularly hard year with the failures because, in those days, that sort of thing happened. You'd expect four or five DNFs in a season at least. The early season wins were probably because other teams had problems or because we managed the tyres. By then, the MP4/3 was becoming old-fashioned because it was more or less an evolution of the 1981 car, whereas the rest of the field had moved on. The step change for McLaren was about to come – in quite a big way.

Official confirmation of that step change had come in the park at Monza on 4 September. Rarely has there been a more awkward or uncomfortable press call. The ambient temperature in the garden of the St George Premier restaurant may have been in the 70s but the atmosphere was chilly as four representatives from Honda sat in garden chairs on a makeshift stage and justified their company's decision to switch the supply of engines to McLaren, even though there was one year left to run in the contract with Williams. Their halting English was heard in stony silence. It was arguably the greatest test of Japanese inscrutability yet devised.

Mr Yoshitoshi Sakurai, managing director of Honda F1, spoke of Honda being 'at the pinnacle' (the pair of Williams-Hondas had, coincidentally, topped the time sheets of first practice that day) and of the need for Honda to put themselves into 'a new challenging situation'. With Williams heading towards a championship Honda desperately wanted to win, such an explanation seemed akin to a golfer spending four years working on his swing and, just on the point of his winning his first Major, changing his grip because it seemed too easy.

There was no doubt that Honda had not been amused when McLaren stole the 1986 championship from Williams at the eleventh hour. And neither had they been impressed when Williams resolutely refused to take on board a Japanese driver (Satoru Nakajima) and then showed no enthusiasm for restraining Mansell at the expense of Piquet, Honda's favoured driver.

All told, the situation had been ripe for Dennis to negotiate a deal for 1988 and beyond. It was his belief that the F1 tempo was changing. Rather than pay for the services of an independent engineering company such as Porsche, the time had come for a committed long-term technical association. Confirmation of the McLaren-Honda partnership had come in a press conference that had looked like a casual garden party but was exactly the opposite.

ALAIN WAS VERY DIFFERENT TO THE DRIVERS I HAD BEEN USED TO IMMEDIATELY BEFORE THAT. FROM MY POINT OF VIEW AS A NEW BOY TO THE TEAM, HE WAS VERY ACCOMMODATING.
NEIL OATLEY

(Left to right) Neil Oatley, Gordon Murray and Ron Dennis keep an eye on progress at the pit wall, the single timing screen and stand rudimentary by today's standards.

Indy Lall

We had not really been aware of the Honda deal until that announcement itself. There had been the usual speculation in the press earlier in the season, but nothing had been confirmed internally at McLaren. In any case, we had been busy just going racing in 1987. It was a much tougher season on the inside than it looked from the outside. This is only a personal feeling but it had looked to me earlier in the season that Alain needed a change. The news of Honda and Alain's new team-mate certainly brought that.

Alain Prost

It's true that I had been talking to other teams in 1987 – but that was no different to any other year because, in truth, the teams were talking to me. I think I had a call from Ferrari every year, starting way back in 1980! But I never had the intention to leave McLaren at any time from when I joined in 1984. Never. The discussion with Honda, in fact, had started at the end of 1986 for 1987 and I don't know exactly what happened at the end of that talk. I remember a meeting with the Honda people in a hotel went on until three or four o'clock in the morning. Everybody was smoking; it was awful for me. That was when we started to have this discussion about who my team-mate should be.

I told Honda that they needed to have the best driver for the future – so it had to be Ayrton. They wanted to have Nelson – and Nelson was a good friend, he was always close to me. I did not know Ayrton very well at the time. But I said, 'Why Nelson? If you want to make a strong team, take the best, take the youngest, the one for the future. Take Ayrton.' It would have been much easier to take Nelson but I don't regret this decision at all. It was right at the time. I always thought about the general interest of the team. McLaren was my family, we were all friends and I'd never had a problem with team-mates before. I was happy with the decision when the official announcement came at Monza in 1987.

Once the Honda officials had stepped awkwardly from the narrow temporary platform in the Monza garden, the stage was literally set for Senna and Prost to step up and shake hands. Given that the season with its existing sponsorship commitments was still in progress, both drivers wore casual clothes free from branding. Their pose – formal rather than effusive – for photographs indicated the start of a journey that, at that stage, looked likely to be difficult rather than dominant.

McLaren would have much to think about, not least designing a car to receive an engine that was not going to last more than 12 months thanks to a ban on turbos for 1989. The thought was that the development of the 1988 engine would tail off as Honda focussed on the V10 for the following season in much the same way that TAG-Porsche appeared to have lost impetus in 1987 as their contract with McLaren reached its final phase. And then there was the question of Prost working with Senna.

Indy Lall

At the end of the last race of 1987 in Adelaide, Ayrton literally stepped out of the Lotus in parc fermé and, still wearing his bright yellow Camel overalls, walked straight into our garage to size up our car. As I said, we'd had a very tough year but you could sense the energy in the team right there and then. It was the end of the season and we were looking forward to the start of the next one. We had this exciting new driver up against Alain, a brilliant driver and a proven quantity. It really was something to look forward to. The guys on the team couldn't wait for 1988.

Ayrton Senna (left) and Alain Prost, appearing slightly apprehensive while wearing 'civvies' at the McLaren-Honda press call at Monza.

Senna was becoming agitated – and Prost knew it. The plan had been for Alain to do the opening tests for the 1988 season in Estoril and Jerez, with Ayrton having his first experience driving for McLaren in the next two tests at Rio and Imola. Alain had no need to be in Brazil. But he was there – sitting in the car Ayrton should have been driving.

Alain Prost *I was obviously aware that Senna was a big name and I wanted to get a first-hand impression of his debut with McLaren. I didn't want to sit at home, waiting for reports from others on how he had coped. I needed to see it for myself. So I went to Rio and I took the opportunity to make the point that we worked as a team because I'd heard that Ayrton liked to have things his own way. I was scheduled to do some laps in the car to check a few things and then hand over to Ayrton for the rest of the test. I completed my laps – as far as I can remember, there were no problems with the car – and came back to the pits, where they began fitting fresh tyres ready for Ayrton. But rather than get out, I stayed in the cockpit for a little while, not saying anything – just sitting there. I could see Ayrton didn't like it because he began pacing up and down. Only when the tyres had been changed and the jacks lowered did I undo the belts and climb out – quite slowly. It was all part of the little games drivers play when the adrenalin starts to flow!*

It is likely that this mind game caused Senna's adrenalin to surge more dramatically than his first experience with the car. This was a test mule; a 1987 MP4/3B with the TAG-Porsche removed and the Honda turbo in its place. By all accounts, it was not a particularly nice car to drive, particularly when compared with what was to come.

The McLaren-Honda MP4/4, being finalised at the team's headquarters in Woking, was about to rewrite the record books and become a classic of its kind. Parked beside its bulky predecessor, the comparison would be stark; a sports car alongside a truck, with the performance to go with it.

Indy Lall *We had this hybrid car from 1987 with a Honda engine. I was running the test team and we had a horrendous time with this car during tests in Brazil. The final test before the first race of the season was held at Imola. While we were there with this awful car, the race team arrived with MP4/4 – and it just looked the bollocks. We were knackered and we were sort of shovelled into the corner because Ayrton didn't want to know about the old car any more – and you can't blame him. But it gives me goose bumps to this day when I think about what happened next. The MP4/4 went on track and the lap times just went quicker and quicker and quicker. It was getting dark – and Ayrton didn't want to stop. It was an absolutely amazing experience.*

Prost begins to learn the ways of Honda during the motor manufacturer's early days with McLaren in 1988.

That performance promise would be backed up when it mattered in the first race in Brazil. Senna would send the local media into raptures when he claimed pole for his first race with McLaren but the pre-race rush to complete the cars (the unfinished spare car being loaded into the hold of the Wednesday night Varig airline flight to Rio) would take its toll when the gear linkage worked loose during the parade lap and forced Ayrton to start from the pit lane in the hastily completed spare car.

Prost had not been without his own troubles. The lack of serious testing was demonstrated during practice by a fundamental weakness in the mounting points for the nose cone. The problem had its lighter side when Alain, with unconscious humour, told journalists, 'I've been 'aving trouble wiz my nuse.' It was an indication of Prost's routinely error-free driving when seasoned observers made a note of the date when Alain actually had a spin. This was due to the laid-back driving position of the MP4/4 compared to the 1987 car, Prost working right up to moments before the start on adjustments to the seat, steering and pedal positions.

Gordon Murray

I'd sat the drivers down and explained the whole concept of the low-line car. Ayrton went, 'Fantastic'. And Alain went, 'Not too sure about that.' Alain had the guys make a seat for him that was a bit more upright and then he complained that he was 150 revs down on the straight relative to Senna. I showed him a picture of his helmet in front of the engine intake. He went back to the more laid-back seat and never mentioned it again. Alain was a bit more, let's say, rigid in his ways.

With drivers like Piquet or Ayrton or Niki [Lauda], anything that looked like an unfair advantage, they would accept with open arms. Alain was more reserved.

Nonetheless, Prost's attention to detail would pay off as, starting from the second row and making full use of the space ahead vacated by Senna, he led the race from start to finish. It was fair reward for the mechanics who had worked until 2 am on Friday, 3 am on Saturday and topped it off with a 5:30 am finish on Sunday. There was just enough time to return to the hotel, shower, change into fresh uniforms and be back at the track in readiness for the race morning warm-up at 8:30 am.

Senna's disqualification from Brazil (the change to the spare car being deemed illegal) was compensated by his first win for McLaren at Imola, with Prost finishing second. There was little to choose between them. And then the scene shifted to Monaco, a circuit on which Senna was determined to make his mark and edge ahead, both physically and psychologically.

The stopwatch would tell the story during qualifying. As would Prost's stunned expression when the times came through.

Neil Oatley

I was running Alain's car. Alain had got down to a 1-minute 26.9-seconds. And then Ayrton produced a 24.4-seconds. Alain improved to a 25.4-seconds – but then Ayrton did a 23.9. I remember a kind of ghostly look came over Alain's face; he just couldn't understand how or where Ayrton's time had come from.

Now all Ayrton had to do was make a clean start and, all things being equal – or as equal as they can be on a track where overtaking is next to impossible – he would win his second race in succession and the Monaco Grand Prix for a second time.

Senna appeared to be on course to do just that, particularly when Prost missed a gear at the start and dropped to third behind a Ferrari. When Alain finally moved into second place with 24 laps

remaining, Ayrton was 49 seconds ahead. Catching the Brazilian, never mind overtaking, was out of the question. But that would not prevent Prost from playing a typically clever card. He set the fastest lap of the race thus far, knowing the news would be relayed to Senna.

Alain Prost

Of course, I knew I had no hope of catching him; particularly Ayrton at Monaco. There was no chance. But in a situation like that, even if you only have a chance in a million, you try to exploit it. I was pushing like crazy and waiting to see what would happen.

Despite pleas from the pit wall, Senna responded. Then he backed off slightly. Whether it was the change in pace or a lapse in concentration, the result was a minor misjudgement that would

have massive consequences. Senna clipped the inside barrier at Portier, the glancing blow being enough to send the red-and-white car across the track and into the Armco on the opposite side. Senna was out and Prost was in the lead; a total disaster for one and a dream result for the other. But the important point at this stage in their relationship was that they remained as friendly as can be expected of two serious rivals within the same team.

Subsequent races would not change the status as the pair took every opportunity, no matter how small, to ease out an advantage. Prost won in Mexico, a necessary result ahead of the two races he liked least; Montreal and Detroit. Finishing second to Senna in each would be as much as Prost could hope for as he remained at the top of the championship.

The sleek lines of the McLaren MP4/4 beautifully profiled as Prost leads Senna at Paul Ricard.

That done, Alain went to his home race, utterly determined to extend his advantage from the moment practice for the French Grand Prix began on Friday 1 July. Fastest on the first day, Alain repeated the trick on Saturday. For the first time in 1988, Senna was not on pole. It was not so much the statistic that mattered, more the manner in which Prost had achieved it. Observers returned from the trackside at Paul Ricard to report that the familiar smooth style had been abandoned, Prost sliding the car and using the kerbs like a man possessed. A half-second advantage over his team-mate proved the effectiveness of Alain's efforts. Could that be carried forward to the 80-lap race?

The answer appeared to be in the affirmative when Prost took the lead and held it, the gap never more than 2.9 seconds but never less than 2.1 seconds. When a backmarker got in the leader's way and Senna closed to 1.1 seconds, Prost put the hammer down once more and pulled away.

Alain Prost

I had to push very hard every lap. With such a short lap [2.369 miles], there were slow cars all the time and I knew Ayrton was very good in situations like that. Also, this was a race with planned tyre stops [there had been none since the Brazilian Grand Prix] and I'd lost races before because of problems in the pits. I wanted time in hand, just in case.

Alain's concern would prove to have substance. Senna, noting that Prost was about to be delayed once more by backmarkers, made his stop at the end of lap 34. Two laps later, Prost came in. At the drivers' briefing, a warning had been issued concerning 'excessive speeding' in the pit lane. This was in the days before mandatory speed limits and electronic timing, a driver's excessive speed being a matter for officials watching in the pit lane. During practice, the McLaren drivers had been singled out for alleged breaches. The threat of a heavy fine appeared to have a bigger effect on Prost during the race as he made more sedate progress than Senna when heading towards the McLaren pit. Added to that, a slow wheel change caused enough of a delay to allow Senna to take the lead as Prost emerged from the pit lane.

The gap was 3.3 seconds as Prost began to slash the deficit, helped by Senna having occasional problems with the manual downshift. By lap 57, Prost was less than a second behind, the McLarens locked in a tense battle as Alain gained under braking, Ayrton having a slight edge on the straights. It was difficult to see Prost finding a way through, given Senna's known superiority when dealing with the consistent challenge of backmarkers (17 of the 26 starters were still running, an impressive survival rate for 1988).

Prost was about to change that preconception in a big way on lap 61 as the leaders came across the fifth-place Lotus-Honda of Nelson Piquet who, in turn, was about to lap a Dallara and a Minardi. Sensing an opportunity, Prost dropped back slightly as they raced full bore along the Mistral Straight towards Signes, Prost then taking the quick right-hander flat out at the very moment Senna was forced to back off slightly. As the mob of cars piled into the braking area for the next corner, the tight right at Beausset, Prost dived down the inside of the unsuspecting Senna. It was a perfectly judged move, to which Senna had no answer either then or, his gearbox problem notwithstanding, during the remaining laps.

Ayrton Senna (left) and Ferrari's Michele Alboreto had to take second best to a supreme Prost in the French Grand Prix.

Neil Oatley

Compared to Ayrton, you have to say that Alain was usually on the back foot for speed. But, in France, he was quick the whole weekend. The move he pulled on Ayrton going into Beausset made quite an impression.

Peter Stayner

I was the wingman for Creighton Brown, who was looking after sponsors and commercial matters for McLaren. After Alain had won that race, we had been out for dinner or a promotion somewhere and I remember we were following Alain's car back to the hotel. When we got there, he drove his car up the steps as far as it would go, right to the front door. Then he jumped out, leapt onto the roof of this hire car and started playing air guitar. He was really happy and I remember thinking, This F1 business is a lot of fun!

That said, Prost's 32nd career win had come at a price, even if he did not realise it at the time.

Neil Trundle

The kerbs at Ricard were red, white, yellow and blue. Alain had been sliding the car over these kerbs lap after lap and the floor was coloured. It looked like a piece of modern art. When we got back to the factory, the floor was scrapped, as usual. I cut out a piece, got Alain to sign it and had it framed.

When Ayrton was chasing Alain, one of the titanium skid blocks had come off Alain's car. It went through the floor of Ayrton's car and punched its way into the cockpit, right by Ayrton's bollocks. He didn't know it was that close, of course, because all he'd felt was a 'Bang!' somewhere underneath. But his car was still going OK, so that was all that mattered.

Alain Prost

Obviously, it was really nice to win that race in France and to beat Ayrton. But during the race I had driven over a kerb and damaged the chassis inside. When we got to the next race [one week later] at Silverstone, the car was understeering and oversteering at every corner. The problem was that we had made changes to the sidepods and other things and it was hard to understand at first exactly what was happening.

Final tweaks to Prost's Honda turbo V6 at Paul Ricard.

Those difficulties would seem minor on race day. The first wet British Grand Prix for 27 years presented problems of a different kind when Prost, unfamiliar with the feel of a carbon clutch in the wet, made a shocking start and found himself engulfed in the spray churned by the midfield runners. This, combined with evil and unpredictable handling, prompted Alain to retire from 16th place after 24 of the scheduled 65 laps. It didn't help that Senna was leading and would go on to win by more than 20 seconds. Prost was duly savaged by the same French journalists who had lavished praise seven days before.

Neil Oatley *The car had been changed quite a lot for Silverstone and it appeared to be worse than it had been when we had tested there not long before. The wind conditions were different but the bottom line was that Alain never felt comfortable. Ayrton could drive a more nervous car whereas Alain liked a bit more understeer. On race day, Alain didn't feel safe in the car and thought he would have an accident if he continued. Credit to him for having the bottle to stand up and be counted. I don't remember any criticism of him in the garage because of his decision to stop.*

Alain Prost *The car still was not correct and I didn't understand why. It was only later that Neil and the mechanics discovered the full effect of what had happened at Le Castellet [Paul Ricard] and why I could not drive the car. When it's wet like this and it's fifth gear, you need confidence. I was losing confidence and the car was going nowhere, so I stopped.*

There were all sorts of stupid comments in the press. Someone even wrote that I was exhausted after winning the French Grand Prix! Other people said I had lost my nerve and couldn't drive in the wet. But I was really good – OK, that's my opinion – when it was wet or slippery. No problem. In fact, I liked it very much when it was like that. But when it was very wet and you have the combination of aquaplaning and visibility, I never wanted to take the risk. I was always thinking of Didier [Pironi] and what happened at Hockenheim [in 1982]. But how do you say that to the press? It's difficult, but I lived with that even though I was losing a little bit of credibility with the press, but not really with the team. As I said at the time, it was my judgement and my life. If people could not accept that view it was their problem.

Prost waits at the pit exit during practice for the German Grand Prix.

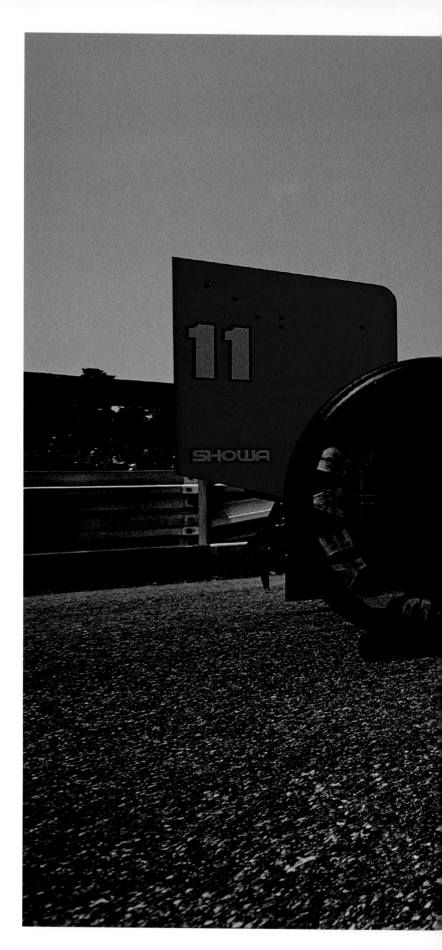

LOOKING BACK, YOU COULD SAY HUNGARY COST ME THE CHAMPIONSHIP.
ALAIN PROST

The ill-informed comments (in French) would continue at the end of the next round at Hockenheim. In a race run in drizzle, Prost spun harmlessly while challenging Senna for the lead. No one could touch Ayrton that day in such conditions and Alain finished just 13 seconds behind and with a faster race lap than Senna. But it meant nothing to detractors, who claimed he was washed up as a race driver.

Alain Prost
I was actually quite happy with second because the race had been run in the wet and I had come back after a bad start. The track was very slippery and my car was set up for dry conditions. OK, I had a small spin, but I don't think anyone else could challenge Ayrton that day. But, of course, the French press weren't interested in that.

Prost finished second to Senna at the Hungaroring but felt he could have won.

Gerhard Berger would finish over half a minute behind in third place, the Ferrari driver commenting that he had been impressed by Prost's speed as the McLaren came by when the rain was at its height. But if Prost was as satisfied as it's possible to be with the runner-up slot in Germany, he was not so happy after finishing in the same position two weeks later in Hungary.

Alain Prost *I know you can say many things about a season of racing – if this or that had happened, the result would have been different – things like this. But, looking back, you could say Hungary cost me the championship. I'd started fifth [unable to find a clear lap in qualifying] and had already tried to take the lead from Senna [but ran wide] when, just as I was about to have another go,*

a front wheel started to vibrate and felt as if it was loose. I eased up and once I realised the problem was not going to get worse, I attacked again. But there was not enough time. I crossed the line half a second behind Ayrton and set the fastest lap. The car felt good originally [the vibration was believed to have been caused by rubber debris picked up when he ran wide]; I should have won.

Prost and Senna were jointly leading the championship with 66 points, Senna moving ahead after winning in Belgium but neither car finishing in Italy, thus denying McLaren a clean sweep in 1988. Prost's struggle into second place at Spa had been caused by incorrect tyre pressures but he would have been in a position to win in Italy (after Senna had collided with a backmarker) had his Honda V6 not suffered a rare failure.

Neil Trundle

Honda ran a different grade of NGK plug at Monza. Why they did it, I don't know. When Alain's engine went onto five cylinders and he came into the pits, we took the engine cover off, out came the plugs – and there it was; the middle had dropped out of one plug. Overheating was the likely cause, which was why we told Ayrton to go rich on the mixture because the wrong grade of plug had been used. With five laps to go, the Ferraris are right on his tail and he gets caught up with a backmarker. If they had changed the plug on Alain's car, I reckon he'd have caught them again. The bit that fell out probably went out the exhaust, so they could have chanced it. The whole thing was very unlike Honda because they rarely – if ever – made mistakes like that. You could say that problem with Alain's engine cost him the championship. Ifs and buts...

Either way, there were just three points separating Prost and Senna with four races to go. Prost moved to the head of the table once more when he won the next race in Portugal and Senna finished sixth. But there was much more to this weekend than the mathematics of the championship. Psychology had been at play in a major way.

The Ferraris of Gerhard Berger and Michele Alboreto were ready to pounce when Prost (right)
had an engine problem and Senna collided with a backmarker at Monza.

With a new chassis at his disposal, Prost felt the car and engine were working better than ever. He proved it by going faster than Senna early in final qualifying and improving on Ayrton's time with apparent ease once Senna had responded. Then came the masterstroke.

With practice having been stopped to allow the recovery of a stricken car, Prost quietly disappeared to the motor home and changed out of his overalls. While Senna waited to go out on his second set of tyres, knowing that the track would be busy during the final 15 minutes, he was deeply unsettled to see Prost, purple

sweater draped across his shoulders, wandering casually through the garage and taking a place on the pit wall, to see how Senna would respond. Prost knew full well that, under such circumstances, the harder Ayrton tried, the slower he would go. Which is exactly what happened although, to be fair to Ayrton, an electrical fault causing the warning lights to flash on and off contributed to the Brazilian losing his rhythm while fighting traffic in addition to his team-mate's deliberate insouciance.

It was harmless gamesmanship – which is more than could be said for what happened in the race as the McLarens started from the

front row for the ninth time in 1988. Senna made the better getaway and turned into the first corner in the lead. It would be for nothing, a collision further behind prompting the red flag.

Now aware of Senna's determination to maintain his lead of the championship, Prost moved further across than before and ran Senna that bit closer to the edge before the Brazilian came through to lead once more into the first corner. Given expected form, that should have been the end of the story as Senna went unchallenged for the rest of the afternoon. But, on 25 September, Prost was wearing his 'Ricard head'.

Making a faster exit through the final corner of the first lap, Prost began to draw alongside Senna as they reached 180 mph on the pit straight – only for Senna to move across and squeeze his team-mate against the pit wall. As startled mechanics whipped their signalling boards out of the way, Prost kept his right foot buried and the momentum going as he eased ahead and edged Senna back across the track in order to take the line into the quick first corner. Job done. Victory number 33 was on its way. And so was the start of a relationship breakdown that, 12 months later, would have disastrous consequences.

Steve Nichols

A lot of people said a lot of things, but I didn't think it was bad. I thought it was race drivers being race drivers. Nobody crashed, nobody died – no harm, no foul – well, maybe there was a little harm. I just thought, 'With two drivers like this in competitive cars, that's what you're going to get.'

Dave Ryan

Estoril was the first time – it seemed to me [as team manager] – that Ron was starting to become pro-Ayrton. Senna was very clever when dealing with Honda. He obviously got on with the Japanese very well but he really worked them 100 per cent to be behind him. I guess Ron must have seen Ayrton as the future but, whatever the reason, there was a shift in the way he dealt with the two drivers. There was no change in the treatment the drivers were receiving. That remained absolutely equal, as it had always been. But Ron's demeanour began to change. And, at the same time, Alain started to become edgy. He began to appear uncomfortable. Meanwhile Ayrton was Ayrton: he was using every tool at his disposal to try and get things his way. That's how we saw it in the garage. We began to realise that all was not as sweet as it could be.

After the race, Prost had a brief but tense discussion with Senna. Ayrton said he had been upset by Alain almost forcing him onto the grass at the second start. Prost said that was the cut and thrust of racing whereas Senna's move on the pit straight was not acceptable. Speaking to the media not long after, Prost said, 'It was very dangerous. I could do nothing. If I'd backed off I might have hit his rear wheel. If we have to take risks like that to settle the World Championship... Well, I don't care about it. If he wants the championship that badly, he can have it.'

Maybe so, but that did not prevent Prost from continuing his roll in Spain, where he led every lap.

Neil Oatley

I don't recall hearing anything going on between the drivers during the post-race debrief in Portugal. They used to get changed in the truck, so maybe it happened there. Whatever may have been said about tactics, Estoril – and also the next one in Jerez – were two races where Alain was definitely quicker. I've no idea why that was.

Prost's win in Spain extended his championship lead to five points, once his lowest scores had been dropped in accordance with the championship structure at the time. In fact, the need for a driver to count only his best 11 results from the 16 Grands Prix would eventually work against Prost.

Two races later, he finished the season with 105 points in total, nine more than Senna and a record at the time. Prost had also won the last race in Australia but the most significant result in championship terms had been a powerful victory for Senna as he recovered from a slow start to win the penultimate round in Japan. Taking the best 11 results into account, Senna became World Champion for the first time on Honda's doorstep and there was nothing Prost could do about it. As far as McLaren were concerned, the season had been close to perfect.

Gordon Murray

From a personal point of view, '88 was a much better year because, unlike '87, the car was all mine; I knew everything about it. I'd been in charge of the design, so I was much more comfortable with '88 as a whole.

I found that Alain was really, really competent. Over the years, I've worked with drivers who are very good at technical feedback and others that don't have a clue. There don't seem to be too many drivers in the middle. There are, however, two types of driver concerning technical feedback. The good ones are the guys who are very, very good at telling you exactly what the car is doing so you can interpret it as a designer. The bad versions of those guys are the drivers that think they know what they should change. Some of them understand and some of them don't. Alain – and Ayrton – used to think about it quite a lot rather than just blurting stuff out. Alain could feel small changes in the car and interpret them very well. Overall, he was pretty good at choosing tyres; he won quite a few races on tyre choice and looking after the tyres. It was one of his strong points.

Prost was not to be denied during the opening lap at Estoril.

Ron Dennis (right) was meticulous in ensuring parity between his two drivers.

Indy Lall *Alain's sensitivity was absolutely incredible. I set up the test team and we used to do extensive mileage in those days. There was a high-mileage test in Jerez; two days with Emanuele Pirro driving and Alain taking over for the third and fourth days. Alain came in after the installation lap as usual and said, 'Something is not quite right on the back.' We checked it over. 'All looks OK to us.' So he said maybe it was just him and he went out again. And came straight back in, saying, 'Something is definitely not right.' It's not often Alain would be as assertive as this, so you knew there had to be something.*

We made a concerted effort; put the set-up wheels on and had a really good look. Sure enough, on the left-rear, we found that where the toe link was on the back of the upright and the outboard rose joint had a reducer sleeve – the sleeve wasn't in there. It had come through from sub-assembly that way and the mechanic had bolted it and torqued it as usual. Spanner checks had been done every night and nothing had been noticed. You couldn't physically move it when we first tried it with the tyre on. Emanuele had driven the car like this for two days and hadn't felt anything. It was almost nothing. But, on the installation lap, Alain had felt it. Absolutely amazing.

Bob Bell *I had joined McLaren at the end of 1982. I was there when Alain came back and for the whole time he was with McLaren. I would have done the aerodynamics: you've got to remember, at the time there was only one aerodynamicist, which was me. In those days you did lots of other stuff, from designing bits of the car to buying the company's first technical computer, setting up R&D; loads of stuff. I rarely went to the races.*

I did quite a few tests when Alain was there. I enjoyed working with him, found him pleasant and pretty easy to work with. Very competent and thoughtful about what he was doing. But since this was never in the heat of the races, it would always be easier in testing. There wasn't the pressure on testing that there is nowadays, it was a more relaxed affair.

But, interestingly, Alain was slightly nervous. He always seemed to be chewing his nails, whereas Ayrton would be the embodiment of calm and superiority. There was a very, very different feel between the two men. Ayrton had a presence that Alain never had, irrespective of the fact that Prost was incredibly successful – a very, very good driver and all of that. But he just didn't seem to have Ayrton's commanding presence. You could imagine in any team that

Ayrton entered he would automatically assume the top rung of the ladder just simply through his presence. It was almost as if he didn't have to do anything.

There's no doubt, however, that Alain had great sensitivity, a great feel for the car. From my experience, he was a bit like Fernando [Alonso] at his best. He could get a car home irrespective of what was happening. He could make it look as if there was nothing wrong with the car. He was particularly good at judging the tyres and getting the best out of them; a very special driver when it came to that.

Neil Trundle *At the end of '87, I had become chief mechanic which meant I was now travelling all the time. I remember we were on £50 a point – and we scored 199 points in '88. It was fascinating to watch these two drivers, so closely matched. Alain never went off, rarely made a mistake, never overdrove the car, never missed a gear. The first corner at Ricard during testing was not far from the pits. You'd hear Ayrton going 'blam-blam-blam' down through the box. Alain would brake hard – you'd hear the revs drop and then, when he was right in the corner, he'd drop down two gears at once. He was as smooth as anything. On the other hand, Alain wasn't changing up at the optimum for the Honda engine. He always seemed to be cautious when revving it and lost a bit of power compared to Ayrton. But, overall, Alain was smart. How he got the speed he did without being aggressive, I really don't know. There's no question he taught Ayrton how to finish races.*

Stefan Johansson *It's probably right to say that being team-mate to Alain was like being at finishing school for any driver. As I said before, I learned a hell of a lot in '87. I'd worked with Senna before [at Toleman] and I knew how he operated. I'm convinced Senna had exactly the same experience I had when he joined McLaren and started working with Prost in '88. But then, as we all know, he started to do his own thing in 1989...*

10. ENOUGH IS ENOUGH

Honda would hold the key – several keys, in fact – for success in 1989. This would be a year of massive technical change as the turbos gave way to normally aspirated engines. There was a fair amount of straw-clutching in season previews when it was suggested that the change of formula would offer teams such as Benetton and March with their Ford and Judd V8s the opportunity to compete on a level playing field.

Not a chance. As soon as the racing got under way, it was clear that the major technical players from Honda, Ferrari and Renault – respectively with V10, V12 and V10 engines – would dominate. The only key question was which of the three would come out on top? And if it was Honda, which of the McLaren drivers would make the best of it? Or, in the minds of some – not least Alain Prost – which driver would be given the best opportunity to win?

Alain Prost

I'd had no problems in 1988. It had been a good season as far as I was concerned, a fair fight between Ayrton and me. But I had noticed a different attitude with Honda. Let's say there were now two separate teams in the garage whereas before there was just the one. At the end of the season I had a meeting with Mr. Kawamoto of Honda in Geneva. I remember it like it was yesterday. It was a strange discussion. I said we had a hard year in 1988 but we did not have any problems with Ayrton. OK there had been tough moments – like Portugal – and I said that, although Ayrton had won more races than me, there had been occasions such as Hungary when I should have won. But no problem, that's part of the game. Above all, I wanted to have the same treatment for both drivers in 1989. I did not want to see an engine come to a race that was special for Ayrton. When you see that as a driver then, psychologically, it's not easy to accept.

Mr Kawamoto said he recognised that. He did not say there had been an advantage but he accepted that Honda had not done a good enough job for me because the engineers were perhaps giving more support to Ayrton. He talked about 'the new generation' of engineers. He told some stories about the way things happen in life and he tried to explain to me that the young guys were an 'after-the-war' generation and they liked the nature of Ayrton because they saw him as being rather like a Samurai. He promised me that it would not be like this any more. I felt confident '89 would be okay. But it turned out to be a disaster.

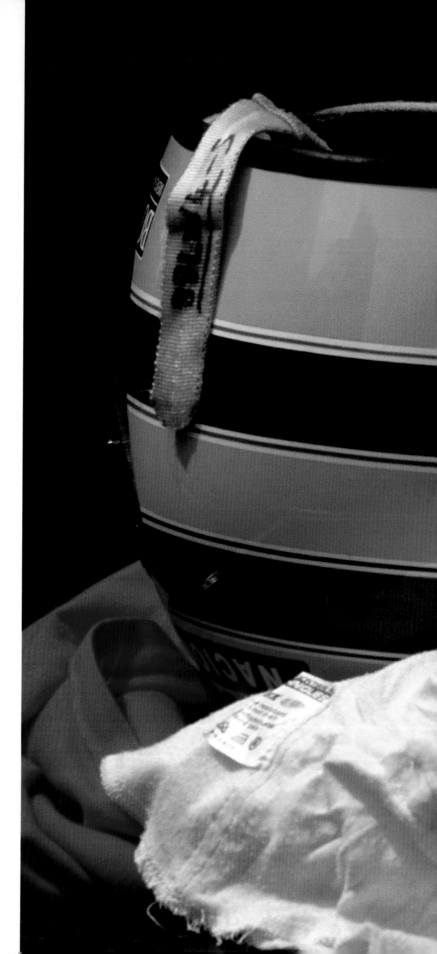

Neil Oatley

When I first came to McLaren, Alain had been there for a long time and, with Stefan as team-mate, Alain was definitely the No 1 driver. Alain was very close to Ron, they had a very good relationship. But there was a step change in the garage when everyone was around Ayrton's car, completely the opposite to how it would have been in '87. It wasn't immediate but it drifted that way very quickly.

Alain found things on a much different level with Ayrton. Alain was used to getting everything done and dusted by 6:30 pm. and then go off with Jacques [Laffite] or French journalists for supper somewhere; whereas Ayrton was this guy spending two hours in the Honda truck. This was in the very early days of having data available for drivers to look at. We didn't have any ourselves as a team, it was all engine data.

Ayrton probably had a mental advantage feeling the Honda people were all his buddies. If the engines were evolving to suit a driving style, inevitably it would be towards Ayrton. Alain was obviously aware of Ayrton's good relationship with Honda and Osamu Goto through his time with Lotus. He was beginning to feel that they might be favouring Ayrton. I'm sure it was psychological. I don't believe Honda – even if they could - would have done something on the engine tuning without us knowing. I couldn't see why they would do that. The engines were always allocated on a lottery. Ron would write the engine numbers on bits of paper, screw them up and put them in each hand. And the drivers chose. It was transparent.

Honda would bring eight of the 3.5-litre V10 engines to each Grand Prix (two for each race car and the spare, plus an additional two as back-ups). The engines were mated to a new, transverse six-speed gearbox at the rear of the latest car. The MP4/5 looked broadly similar to its predecessor but incorporated the usual aerodynamic improvements, greater cooling and air induction to cater for the naturally aspirated engine.

It had been the familiar last-minute rush to meet the deadline for the first race in Brazil on 26 March. For the second year in succession, Senna started from pole and failed to win, his dream of victory at home shattered on this occasion by a collision with Berger's Ferrari at the first corner.

Prost would finish second with a brilliant job of damage limitation. Having led briefly just before his first pit stop, Alain discovered that a deterioration of the clutch became so bad that he would have to make the second set of tyres last the distance rather than risk getting stuck trying to leave the pits after another stop. He crossed the line, fending off the March-Judd of Mauricio Gugelmin.

Out front, and not expecting to be there, was Nigel Mansell, as he celebrated a move from Williams to Ferrari in a car that hitherto had been unable to string together more than a handful of laps before the revolutionary paddle-shift gearbox gave trouble. Already, McLaren's chances of a clean-sweep in 1989 were gone. Such thoughts would seem a luxury when more pressing internal matters arose at the next race.

Starting from the front row at Imola and lapping the entire field on their way to finishing first and second, Senna and Prost may have depressed those hoping Brazil had marked an end to McLaren's monopoly. But almost as soon as the San Marino Grand Prix had ended, a crack appeared in the red-and-white armoury. Prost collected his trophy and walked out, brushing aside the official press conference (which would later attract a $5,000 fine) without pausing to speak to the French media.

ALAIN WAS USED TO GETTING EVERYTHING DONE AND DUSTED BY 6:30 PM; WHEREAS AYRTON WAS THIS GUY SPENDING TWO HOURS IN THE HONDA TRUCK.
NEIL OATLEY

In the absence of any comment from the team, journalists were left to draw their own conclusions from what they had seen on the racetrack. Senna had taken the lead from the start and pulled out 2.7 seconds on Prost in the first three laps. At the start of lap four, Berger had smashed into the same wall Senna would hit fatally at Tamburello corner five years later, the Ferrari quickly engulfed in flames. Such an unexpected sight – and the initial thought that the driver was trapped in the cockpit – prompted the red flag. Berger survived with nothing more than light burns to his hands. The same could not be said for a smouldering relationship that was about to burst into metaphorical flames.

It later transpired that Senna, anxious to avoid the sort of first corner collision that had cost him dearly in Brazil, had suggested it would be foolish for the McLaren drivers to race each other. He had proposed that whoever made the best start should remain

unchallenged into and through Tosa, the corner at the end of the long straight. Prost had duly abided by the agreement.

Assuming the deal would be the same at the restart, Prost made the better getaway and led through Tamburello and on towards Tosa. That seemed to be that. Except that Ayrton had other ideas and rushed into the space Prost, in his innocence, had left available as he took the normal racing line into Tosa. Senna assumed the lead and, with it, any hope of the McLaren drivers ever working together again.

Alain Prost *I saw him on the left and there was plenty of space and I thought, it's OK, I'll take the normal line to make a better exit – and he overtook me.*

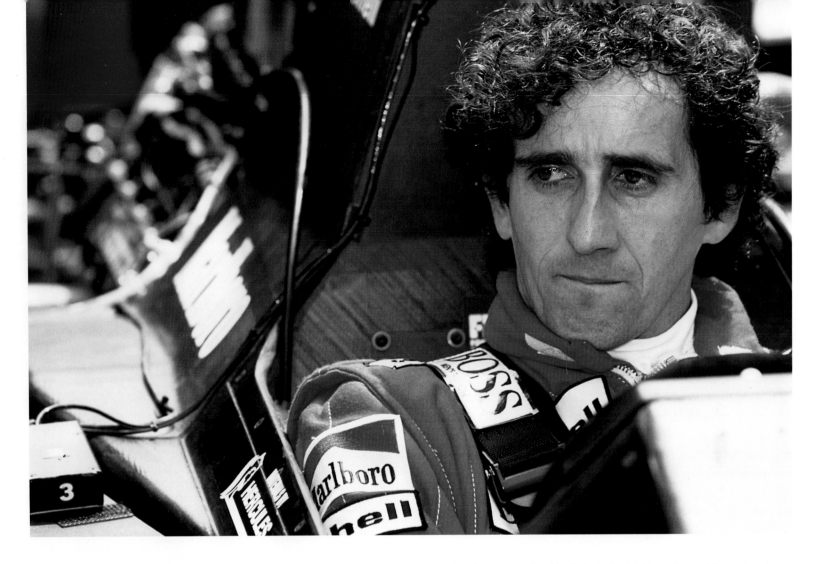

Senna lays down a marker by taking the inside line into Tosa at Imola, giving Prost much pause for thought. It would permanently change the dynamic of their relationship.

Word of the agreement filtered out during the next few days. By the time the teams had gathered at Monaco less than two weeks later, talk of a damaging split within McLaren was high on the media agenda. Sensing trouble, Ron Dennis called a press conference and explained that he had known nothing about the private agreement between his drivers. He said Ayrton had been forced to apologise to Alain, all was well with the world and it would be nice if the media would stop writing stories to the contrary. Dennis's optimism had been based on a head-to-head discussion with his drivers at a test session at Pembrey. Making a special trip by helicopter to the club circuit in Wales, an angry Dennis had marched Senna and Prost into the team's minibus and demanded an explanation. At the end of a tense exchange, Dennis made it clear that no driver was bigger than the team.

I THOUGHT, IT'S OK, I'LL TAKE THE NORMAL LINE TO MAKE A BETTER EXIT – AND HE OVERTOOK ME.
ALAIN PROST

Neil Oatley

It was unusual for Ron to turn up to a test like this without good reason, so we knew something was going on – but we had no idea what that might be. From our point of view, the test seemed normal. I remember we all sat at a picnic bench eating fish and chips. Although we obviously didn't realise it at the time, that was probably the last time the drivers spoke to each other.

Steve Nichols

I was Ayrton's race engineer but knew nothing about the agreement. I had a little bit of sympathy with him and what you might call a very technical get-out clause in that this had been a restart, so all bets were off. On the other hand, if you make an agreement, then stick to it. Ayrton got a good run at Alain [into Tosa]. He was alongside, sitting there thinking, What do I do? You know that's not in his psyche. But, if you made an agreement – then, yes, you do lift.

Alain Prost

In the meeting with Ron, I did not talk. I just listened. Ron asked Ayrton if there had been an agreement and he said 'Yes', there was, but only for the first start, not for the second'. But, more important, he said I had overtaken him! I said, 'I don't know how many million people had seen what happened on television'. He had overtaken me and this was not what we had agreed. It took maybe 20 minutes before Ayrton would accept what had happened. It was unbelievable.

Senna, refusing to speak any longer about Prost at Monaco, does his talking by leading on the track.

Prost and Senna talk to their engineers at Monaco –
but not to each other.

Jean-Louis Moncet

In the beginning, the French journalists could see the atmosphere between Senna and Prost was very good. But then it changed at Imola. Alain asked Johnny Rives [motor sport correspondent for L'Equipe] and I to go with him on his jet to the test in Wales. On the way back, he talked to us about the deal with Senna at Imola. He said that Ron had been really upset and he was very, very hard with Ayrton. He had said to Ayrton, 'If you have a deal, you must respect it.' Alain told us that Senna was crying. Then Johnny wrote the story.

Dennis had finished his press briefing at Monaco by denying there was a rift within the team: 'It's not right that we should be portrayed this way,' said Dennis. 'McLaren likes to have fun while racing.'

Dennis was hard-pressed to see the funny side when L'Equipe hit the streets the morning after he had told the media all was sweetness and light. Prost, who claimed he had been speaking off the record to Rives, was quoted as saying: 'I do not wish to drag McLaren into difficulties caused by the behaviour of Senna. McLaren has always been loyal to me. At a level of technical discussion, I shall not close the door completely but for the rest I no longer wish to have any business with him. I appreciate honesty and he is not honest.'

Senna, deeply upset by the story, was just as forthright with his response. 'I am persuaded that in acting like that Alain wanted to implicate me, make me carry the can, make me culpable, in a phrase: put pressure on me,' said Ayrton. 'Since that day [publication of the interview] it's finished. I don't want to hear any more talk about that guy.'

Neil Oatley

From that moment, there was no conversation between the two drivers for the rest of the season. In the debrief room, there would be the two drivers, Gordon Murray and two engineers – Steve Nichols and myself. Ayrton would ask me questions about what our car was doing and Alain would ask Steve. Occasionally they could manage a 'Hello', but that was the limit of their communication. Apart from that, the rest of the team was immune to what was going on between the two drivers although I'm sure Ron was getting it in the ear from both of them.

Dave Ryan

I think the arrival of Ayrton was the first time Alain's status had been seriously challenged on a performance level and you could see Ayrton became a bit edgy because he knew Alain was his biggest challenger. Ayrton did things in a different way. He was a brilliant driver, but very complex in the way he dealt with things. It started out amicably enough but then it became intense rivalry. I wasn't dealing with them from a management point of view. I just had to make sure we did the best we could in the garage and deal with everything absolutely fair and square. But it was pretty obvious towards the end that things were very fractious.

We managed the garage very well. It was always one team servicing the two cars. Each car had its own crew but when one car had a lot of work on it, the other crew would come over and help and I managed to keep everything on a pretty even keel. It was the same when it came to pit stops. It was just one of our cars coming in. What happened on the circuit was nothing to do with us.

Gordon Murray

I loved working with those two because they were two very technical drivers, which meant you had two sets of information coming in. They were both good and technical but they were different. Prost used to analyse everything and then he and the team and the engineer on his car would make a decision based on that. Senna used to think a hell of a lot about what was about to happen and sit down to think of the best way of handling it. But I didn't favour anybody. I wanted to win championships, that's all. There was very little chat between the two of them at this point in any case. But at least everything was out in the open.

Bob Bell *I had very little involvement in the Senna versus Prost thing because most of the rivalry between them happened on the track. I saw very little of that simply because it was not the sort of thing you would have seen in the factory when, occasionally, they would have been there, or at the test track. Could be a false view of the situation simply because of the relationship I had with it at the time, but I look back on that era with a lot of fondness in as much as I didn't see evidence of the full-on war that people talk about now. I saw great rivalry between them, but I also saw great respect and a sense of fun in the whole thing. For a long time Ron, Ayrton and Alain had an ongoing situation where they were playing practical jokes on each other. I don't think of it as badly as it's been portrayed.*

I recall a test at Imola. Ron had flown in to make a sponsor presentation somewhere. He'd had the car liveried and was taking photos in the garage before dashing off. When Ron wasn't looking, Alain got hold of the camera, popped into the loo, dropped his trousers, photographed his arse and returned the camera, hoping that these things would be printed off and distributed without Ron checking them first. I don't know what happened in the end but it says a lot about Alain. It was part of the practical joking that went on.

But when on track and the red mist came down that was a different thing. It's true of all racing drivers, particularly team-mates in a situation where either of them can win the championship and they're going head-to-head in the same car. That happens. They were both very intense from that point of view. But I saw another side of it. I saw camaraderie, I saw humour. I don't recall any animosity in the team from either side of the garage towards one another. There was great rivalry between the engineers – but a friendly rivalry.

Neil Oatley *It didn't really affect the rest of the team. The intensity of their relationship didn't spill over. As far as we were concerned, it was a good fight for the championship because, fortunately, we were reasonably dominant.*

That domination would continue at Monaco, Senna winning despite losing first and second gears. He mentioned this at the post-race press conference and explained how he managed to maintain lap time without giving the game away. The look on Prost's face said everything about his error in giving up serious pursuit after being at a standstill

for 20 seconds when Piquet's Lotus and the Dallara of an outraged Andrea de Cesaris collided and blocked the track at Loews.

The McLaren drivers left Monaco equal on points, the championship lead see-sawing as Senna won in Mexico (Prost making a rare error of judgement with tyre choice and finishing fifth). Prost then took his turn in the United States Grand Prix. Senna had led the race on the streets of Phoenix until half-distance before an electronics problem sent him into the pits. If he thought that retirement was frustrating, much worse was to follow two weeks later in Canada.

Nineteen of the 26 starters failed to reach the finish of a wet race on Circuit Gilles Villeneuve. Among the retirements were both McLarens; the first time this had happened since Monza the previous year. Prost lasted for just two laps before a pick-up point failed on the front suspension. Senna, meanwhile, produced a superb comeback drive after two perfectly timed stops for dry and then wet tyres to retake the lead and pull away. The Brazilian was in

a league of his own. Three laps from the end, the Honda V10 blew up as he passed the pits for the 66th time.

This was the first such failure Senna had suffered during his three years with Honda. If he was justifiably feeling sorry for himself, it was perhaps just as well he couldn't hear the loud cheers in the media centre when the camera showed the McLaren parked with smoke billowing from the airbox. Prost still led the championship by two points.

He also led the motor sport columns with speculation over his future. Another year with McLaren had been in doubt from the moment he stormed out of the paddock at Imola. Mansell had confirmed he was staying for a second season with Ferrari and the sensible money was on Prost finally succumbing to what had become an annual offer from Maranello. His home Grand Prix would surely be the place to put these rumours to bed.

Calling a press conference at Paul Ricard, the top sportsman in France and by then holder of the Legion d'Honneur, addressed his audience in English. The howls of protest could be heard outside the interview room. And the louder the dissent, the more Alain seemed to enjoy it before finally switching from the common language of F1 to his native tongue. Regardless of the language, he actually said very little, other than the fact that he would not be driving for McLaren in 1990.

If anything, Prost merely succeeded in accelerating speculation rather than stopping it. Paddock gossip included a Marlboro-sponsored car designed by Barnard (about to leave Ferrari) and powered by Renault. Or there was the possibility of Ferrari or Williams-Renault. Or one year's sabbatical. Meanwhile, Alain got on with what he did best by winning in France and then at Silverstone.

Only a couple of months before, few would have bet on Prost leading the championship by 20 points come the halfway point in the season. Even fewer would have reckoned on Senna retiring from four races on the trot (transmission in France and a spin into a gravel trap at Silverstone).

Prost was on course to extend his lead even further when he had the measure of Senna at Hockenheim. Then sixth gear broke three laps from home and Ayrton gratefully surged through to collect three more points than his team-mate. If nothing else, the McLaren-Honda domination of the German Grand Prix cast doubt in Prost's mind over the wisdom of walking away at the end of the season from the most competitive car.

Close friends reported that he appeared preoccupied two weeks later in Hungary. If he hadn't decided where to go in 1990, then the choice would be confused by the Williams-Renault of Riccardo Patrese taking pole and leading the first two-thirds of a race that was eventually won by Mansell's Ferrari. But at least Prost continued to head the championship after finishing fourth at the Hungaroring, two places behind Senna. He was behind Ayrton again at Spa-Francorchamps, Senna leading a McLaren one-two after excelling on a track made even more tricky by wet, cool conditions.

Two weeks later at Monza, the ambient temperature was hot but the atmosphere on one side of the McLaren garage was profoundly chilly. On the Wednesday before the Italian Grand Prix, Prost had signed a 66-page contract committing him to Ferrari for 1990 and beyond. The unhappy news that he was ending a six-year association was not improved by the thought that Prost would be taking McLaren's secrets to their greatest rival.

Prost was under no illusions about how McLaren might feel. And neither was there any doubt – in his mind at least – that the treatment from Honda might be less than equitable from here on in. That feeling of persecution would be fed by events during practice and become public in the post-race press conference. The fact that Prost had actually won the race almost seemed irrelevant in the flow of innuendo.

'All I want,' said Prost, 'is to be able to compete against Ayrton Senna with the same equipment. I can't understand why we can't have the same treatment. Ayrton was *two seconds* quicker than me during qualifying – can you believe that? I've had the same engine problems all weekend – and with two different engines. I've complained about it but nothing was done. I don't feel confident for the rest of the season.'

The irony was that while Prost was airing his grievances, Senna's car was being wheeled into the paddock with the engine bay covered with Shell oil that ought to have been inside the V10. Senna had led from the start – the manner in which he had pulled away being another cause for complaint from Prost – only to have a massive engine failure with fewer than nine laps to go.

Prost's post-race comments may have been doing little for his relationship with the team but his actions not long before had sent his declining friendship with Dennis spiralling towards rock bottom. While standing on the podium, Alain had been overwhelmed by the reaction from the crowd beneath as they swamped the track in the customary Monza manner and welcomed the new 'Ferrarista'. On a sudden impulse, Prost had leaned over the railing and dropped his trophy into the hands of disbelieving fans.

Dennis was aghast. His drivers were contractually bound to give their trophies to the team. In a fit of pique, Ron dashed his winning constructor's cup at Prost's feet and stormed off. Six years before at Monza, while driving for Renault, Prost had needed shielding from a hostile crowd. Now he almost needed protection from his own team.

Ron Dennis *Since the very beginning of the acquisition of McLaren, we started to keep the trophies with the driver having a replica. But the trophies belonged to the team. The Monza situation was particularly upsetting for me. By this time, Alain just couldn't cope with Ayrton in the other car and had decided to go to Ferrari. So, you had the euphoria of having won the race and the tifosi at his feet. In a moment of weakness, Alain chose to throw his trophy to the crowd, which I saw as the ultimate insult because he was giving something that didn't belong to him to the very people who represented the most competitive team we were trying to beat. I thought that was incredibly disrespectful. Alain later commissioned a replica to be made and he came and apologised. But, in truth, it took time to get over this because it was distressing. Winning races is tough enough and trophies are the spoils of war, as it were.*

Alain Prost *Things became very tense in 1989. The business with the cup: it was not premeditated. I had just signed with Ferrari, I had won the race and thousands of people were in front of me and all around. To be honest, I don't know what happened. Giving them the cup was like a sort of present. But Ron was so upset… so* upset. I could understand this later on. When you have tough years like this and tough relationships, you sometimes lose your judgement – I'm talking about myself, not anybody else. You have people like Jo Ramirez [team co-ordinator] or some of the engineers trying to keep the stability. Otherwise, you do things from your heart – but you don't know what you are doing. For Ron, the trophies are very important because they represent the history of the company. So you had this and the fact that we were in Italy, he was losing one of his drivers to Ferrari – and that driver had won the race. I can understand his upset. But I did not do it on purpose at all. Of course, we could never get the trophy back but years later I had a copy made and presented it to Ron during a nice evening at the McLaren factory.*

For the remainder of 1989, however, 'nice evenings' would be hard to find at McLaren, certainly not after the next race in Portugal. A McLaren may have finished second at Estoril but it was driven by the man due to leave the team. Even worse, Senna's McLaren had finished its race with the right-rear wheel hanging off due to an argument with Mansell over who should be leading, a clash that could have been prevented by better communication between pit and driver.

Prost led Senna by 24 points, the margin being reduced when Senna led every lap of the Spanish Grand Prix. Given that drivers could only count their 11 best results from 16 races, it made for a complicated but none the less intriguing situation going into the penultimate race in Japan.

Prost, having finished in the points 13 times thus far, would need to drop his two worst scores. He had won four races compared to six for Senna but the important fact was that Ayrton had managed to score points on just seven occasions. In other words, every single point he could grab in Japan and Australia would count. Or, to put it more dramatically, if Senna won these two races, the championship would be his, regardless of where Prost finished. That would have a crucial effect on the outcome of the Japanese Grand Prix.

Prost, aware of Senna's probable mindset, let Dennis know how he intended to deal with it.

Alain Prost *I told Ron that too many times in the past Senna had pushed the situation – pushed his luck – and only my action by opening the door had prevented an accident. I said I was not going to do that again because we were fighting for the championship. If Ron wanted to tell this to Ayrton, that was up to him. I said I would prefer to lose the championship rather than back off. I had had enough.*

John Hogan *I think Alain handled his situation in a very equitable way. He wasn't excited about it at all. Senna was the one trying to put the pressure on all the time because that's the sort of guy Ayrton was. He didn't want any competition out of the team or in the team – or anywhere on the track. Prost came at it from the standpoint that you've got to beat everybody on the track so you might as well have him in the same car. That was his approach, but then it became acrimonious. Imola was the beginning of the end, so to speak.*

Alain had come to me at the British Grand Prix, saying, 'Ayrton's fucking mad.' When I asked why, he said, 'He's surging on the straight. I don't know what he's trying to do. It's just weird.' He didn't brake-test him but Ayrton was surging the throttle so Prost couldn't get into his rhythm. Ayrton was interrupting Prost's style as much as anything because he knew that Alain was as smooth as anything in the way he drove.

Prost had also made his thoughts known to a few members of the media whom he trusted and knew would not sensationalise the point before the race. Prost may have wanted to put this on record but such a dramatic statement from the normally restrained Frenchman also suggested it might be inevitable.

Initially, the thought seemed irrelevant when Senna took his 12th pole of the season. But, when Prost was faster during the race morning warm-up, it was clear he had a plan. Part of his strategy was to run with less rear wing, and to have a straight-line speed advantage in this certain fight with his team-mate.

The dispute between the McLaren drivers reached its worst possible conclusion with a collision at Suzuka. Prost has already vacated the cockpit while Senna is pushed back, ready to rejoin the Japanese Grand Prix in a contentious manner.

The race plan got off to a perfect start in every sense when Prost, taking advantage of the outside of the front row being on the racing line, immediately got ahead of Senna as they raced downhill towards the first corner. Now there were just the remaining 193 miles to deal with.

For more than 40 laps, Prost would command this race. Occasionally he would back off slightly and Ayrton would close, only for Alain to ease ahead once more. But then Senna made a huge effort.

Neil Oatley *Alain had pulled something like five seconds in front and it looked like he was fairly comfortable, but then Ayrton started to pull it back. The gap went from 4.6 seconds to 1.8 seconds in a ten-lap period.*

With six laps remaining, Senna prepared to attack on the approach to the final chicane.

Alain Prost *Ayrton came from very far back and I didn't see him immediately. At that chicane, as it was then, it was almost impossible to overtake in a normal situation. By the time I saw him I had already started to turn in. This time I did not leave the door open. It was not done on purpose – I was turning into the corner as I normally would but it was not in my interest to make a crash. I had thought mainly about the race during practice and qualifying, and I had been eight-tenths quicker in the warm-up. Once I'd made the good start, I knew for sure I could win. Yes, I also knew Ayrton had to win the race but I did not want the championship to finish like this. Not at all. I was so disappointed because I was going to win this race.*

It wasn't a collision in the sense of broken suspension and flying carbon fibre: more a silly slow-motion end to an enthralling high-speed contest between two of the best drivers in the world. The sad denouement continued as, with wheels interlocked, they stumbled to a silent halt in the middle of the entry to the chicane.

Neil Oatley *Standing in the pits and seeing both cars go off was the worst nightmare. Alain is not a dirty driver but on that occasion he, let's say... didn't do it very well.*

John Hogan *Alain was a bit clumsy, but he'd had enough. I think that's a good summary of it. He was talking about being intimidated, which was the tactic that Senna adopted once he realised he couldn't outdrive Prost, so he had to adopt Plan B. And Plan B was to intimidate as much as he could and he kept that going every time they were on the track. I think Alain finally said to himself, Enough's enough. If I'm going, you're coming with me. Trying to apportion blame for the Suzuka incident is a waste of bloody time because you can see it from both points of view. But I think you've got to look at the bigger picture and ask, what was Senna trying to do? He was trying to intimidate Prost, and Prost said he wasn't going to be intimidated. The whole thing was inevitable.*

Prost, believing his suspension had been damaged, evacuated the cockpit and walked quickly away. Senna, with goodness knows what racing through his mind, simply wanted to get going again. With Prost out of the reckoning, the championship remained possible.

As the marshals untangled the cars, Ayrton frantically gestured to be pulled back. Once this was done, Senna was now ready for a push-start, a perfectly legal move since the McLaren was in the middle of the track and clearly in a dangerous position. Ayrton then negated that push-start proviso by steering straight into the escape road rather than following the course of the track. The legality of the assisted start was put into further question when, with the V10 now running, he rejoined by driving through the escape road exit and bypassing the chicane completely.

He was no longer leading, of course, but it was still game-on even though, as he started lap 48, Senna was aware all was not well with the front of his car, a handicap made worse when the nose wing eventually flew off and prompted a pit stop. In a characteristic comeback, Senna drove like a man possessed and retook the lead from the Benetton-Ford of Alessandro Nannini with three laps to go.

By now the political wheels in the paddock were moving swiftly into top gear. Driven by the less than impartial and difficult to ignore FISA president, Jean-Marie Balestre, decisions were being made which would lead to Senna's exclusion from the results. McLaren immediately lodged an appeal that would be rejected in Paris a week later.

To all intents and purposes, Prost had become 1989 World Champion the moment the stewards had reached their verdict as darkness closed in at Suzuka on 22 October. It was an extremely messy and unsatisfactory way to win his third title.

In the meantime, there was still work to be done on track at the final round in Australia. Against an endless schedule of interviews, statements and media calls focussed almost exclusively on Senna and McLaren, there was a sense of relief when the 41 entries got down to business and pre-qualifying began on the Friday morning in Adelaide.

As for qualifying proper, there were no surprises when the McLarens filled the front row. Having been beaten by Prost on the first day and claiming that he was held up by his team-mate, Senna smashed Prost's best lap on the second day and really got rid of his frustration by going quicker still to establish pole with a time eight-tenths faster than anyone else.

All of that appeared largely irrelevant when rain began to fall on race morning and would not let up until the evening. A 30-minute delay to the scheduled start signalled the beginning of a predictable pantomime. Drivers were milling about on the grid, some in conversation with their team managers, others discussing with each other the possibility of refusing to race because of standing water that was not draining quickly enough from the street circuit.

As Senna sat impassively in his car, waiting to start, there was no need to ask Prost what his feelings were. He had made these known at Silverstone the year before and the conditions in Adelaide were ten times worse. Prost would complete one lap, pull into the pits and climb from a McLaren for the last time. In the opinion of many, and in the face of most drivers having continued racing despite threatening to stop, Prost's was the bravest decision of the weekend.

By the time the race had been stopped for good after Senna had smashed into the back of a Brabham hidden by the spray from another car, Prost had already left the track. After six years, 30 wins, 458 points and three World Championships, it was a sad way to end his partnership with McLaren. But good memories would endure.

Prost takes the downhill walk back towards the pits and the 1989 title at Suzuka.

Dave Ryan *I thought Alain was fantastic, certainly one of the better team members I've ever worked with in terms of respect in the garage. I can't think of a negative at all. I could sit down and tell you things about Ayrton, Keke, Wattie, all the guys. But with Alain, it was just a nice experience. He was a good guy, quick to praise the guys around him. Perhaps he didn't handle the Ayrton situation particularly well; perhaps he let it get on top of him because his demeanour certainly changed. Sometimes you would be aware of the perception that he was a bit spoiled, that he couldn't accept being beaten. But the reality is, he was probably hard done by. Saying that, he never complained to the guys in the garage. When he was with us, he did his job. But as 1989 went on, we could see he was no longer the bubbly guy he had been. There was a definite change. The time with Ayrton left its mark.*

Alain Prost *I had some difficult times, for sure. But, overall, I was very happy at McLaren. I don't regret the decision to suggest [in 1987] that Ayrton should join the team. As I said before, it was right at the time. Maybe without Ayrton, I could have had another two or three championships. But that doesn't matter. With the history we made, I believe we took F1 to a different level. Anyway, it was to be much later that I began to understand what racing with and against Ayrton really meant. First, though, we were to have the experience of 1990.*

Momentary and close dispute between the McLaren drivers at the start of the very wet Australian Grand Prix, Senna (right) going on to lead and eventually collide with a backmarker, Prost stopping after one lap and climbing from his McLaren for the last time.

11. THE ITALIAN JOB

On Tuesday 13 February, just over three weeks before the 1990 F1 season was due to begin, Nigel Mansell held a pre-season press conference in Pimperne in England's Dorset countryside. Such a modest location to discuss a major international sport story was dictated by Nigel's latest acquisition. Mansell had chosen the English village to locate a garage and showroom dealing in new and used Ferraris. With Prancing Horse emblems on the wall, the dealership was a proud badge of office to celebrate his forthcoming second season with the iconic team. It was also a handy way to show off a Ferrari 640, the very car with which he had won the previous year's Hungarian Grand Prix.

This car, with 27 on the nose, was neither on loan nor a show car. It belonged to Mansell as part of his deal to accept equal status with Alain Prost for 1990. The concession on Nigel's part said as much as Ferrari's rare decision to let one of their recent F1 cars out of captivity.

Mansell had every reason to look pleased as, dressed in a smart suit and Ferrari tie, he welcomed the British F1 press. He was relaxed and cheerful thanks to 1,500 miles of testing that had gone well. And Nigel being Nigel, he was confident he could beat Alain, even if he did not say as much over a cup of tea in his office. But you could tell by his demeanour that a year at Maranello had given Mansell a head start. Never

mind Prost's three world titles to none for Mansell – the only difference between the two drivers as far as Nigel was concerned would be their physical size.

Nigel Mansell *I'd never truly appreciated just how small Alain was. I remember during testing that I'd tried to get into his car – and couldn't. And when he got into mine, he could barely see over the steering. There was something like a 15-inch difference in the pedal reach. The problem was it would take about 45 minutes to convert the cars and, when you've only got one T-car, that was going to be a drama if the spare car wasn't set up for you. We'd worked out, for example, that Alain could have the T-car for France and it would be for me at the next race, which happened to be Silverstone, so that was OK. But you just had to hope there were no unexpected problems if it wasn't your turn.*

But, apart from that, I was happy to have Alain as team-mate. It was going to provide a good yardstick. I did get to try his car [once it had been converted] during testing at Estoril and found I couldn't get on with it at all. We worked out that because I was so much taller there was a lot more weight at the front of the car so we had to stiffen the front springs. It was OK after that – but you wouldn't have thought it would make that much difference. I mean, the thing was undriveable beforehand as far as I was concerned.

Nigel Mansell and Alain Prost: differences in size and attitude.

Mansell's confidence had been bolstered by a year in which he was 'The Man' at Ferrari. His relationship had got off to a dream start with the unexpected victory in Brazil. After a swashbuckling win in Hungary, Nigel was being hailed as '*Il Leone*' (The Lion) by the fickle but, for now, adoring *tifosi*. He could see no reason why that should not continue. But it did not take into account the diligence of his new team-mate. Prost had already started preparations for 1990 by persuading Steve Nichols to make the move from Woking to Maranello.

Steve Nichols

It was when we were in Adelaide for the last race of '89 that Prost called and asked to meet in his room. He said he was going to Ferrari and he wanted me to come with him. That was a pretty nice thing to be asked because, when you think about it, for the whole time I'd been at McLaren with Alain, I'd never been his engineer. Obviously, we'd worked together in the debriefs and I guess he must have liked the way I went about it. It was kind of hard to turn down because it was such a compliment from what, in my book, is one of the very best drivers there has ever been.

John Hogan

Although Marlboro obviously had strong connections with Ferrari as well as McLaren, Alain's move to Maranello was largely of his own volition. They were after him and we certainly wouldn't have had strong objections to that. The point to remember is that when the negotiations started, John [Barnard] was there and he thought Alain was the best ever.

Barnard's undoubted respect for Prost was not enough to prevent him leaving Ferrari and accepting a new challenge with Benetton just as the 1989 season was ending. Prost had joined on condition of Barnard being present. He could have torn up the contract but didn't. Such is the romantic lure of Ferrari, even for a reasonably dispassionate driver such as Prost.

In November of that year, Nichols found himself taking on a Barnard project for the second time. As before, he could see no sense in making change for change's sake, the Ferrari 641 being a logical development of the previous year's car.

Testing, as Mansell pointed out to the British media, had proved the few developments to be effective and he was raring to go. So was Prost. The previous season may have brought the championship but the conclusion had been far from satisfactory. He immediately tapped into the boundless potential at Ferrari. Prost's aura of success and professionalism had an immediate reciprocal effect. They were ready for the United States Grand Prix on 11 March 1990. Prost was mildly amused in Phoenix when he and the rest of the F1 establishment witnessed mounting frenzy as everyone waited to see if Senna was actually going to turn up. This race would mark the end of an off-season in which the only beneficiaries appeared to have been the manufacturers of fax paper.

FISA had issued endless press releases demonstrating increased levels of indignation over Senna's refusal to rescind claims that the governing body had manipulated the 1989 World Championship in favour of Prost. There was an apology of sorts and Senna duly received his 1990 licence at the 11th hour and went on to win in Phoenix after an entertaining fight with the nimble Tyrrell-Ford of Jean Alesi. With Gerhard Berger having started from pole (before hitting the barrier during the race), McLaren appeared to be back in the old routine despite hugely time-consuming politics during the European winter.

The Ferrari garage, by comparison, was a shambles, the disintegrating optimism exacerbated by the unfulfilled promise of testing. Mansell started from 17th place, his practice disrupted by the semi-automatic gearbox either selecting the wrong gear or no gears at all. Hydraulics were to blame; specifically, the tank was found to be porous and leaking hydraulic fluid into the engine oil. This tank, not having been tested before, was discarded and the old design brought from Italy as hand luggage in time to be installed for the race. The effort would be in vain when Prost's car deposited most of its hydraulic fluid around the track, prompting retirement after 20 of the 72 laps.

Mansell's departure was more theatrical. The clutch exploded and fractured an oil line, causing a flash fire and seizing the engine. Nigel being Nigel, the spectacle had occurred when at speed on the straight and, with appropriate drama, he somehow avoided contact with the concrete walls lining the street circuit.

The mood in Maranello was unlikely to have been improved when they heard Ron Dennis comment that Ferrari may have won the winter Grand Prix but not the important one that followed. The remark may have been tongue-in-cheek but what Dennis had to say two weeks later in São Paulo on the subject of Nichols' remuneration had more of a barbed and personal intent.

One way or another, money was on everyone's mind in Brazil. The country's new president had chosen to put the brakes on rampant inflation just a few days before the Grand Prix. He did it by freezing the economy. It didn't matter how much money you had in the bank; you couldn't get at it. A knock-on effect of the absence of hard currency in circulation meant visitors could not change US dollars – normally

the passport to everything in Brazil. The F1 teams had their negotiating feet cut from under them, an unusual and uncomfortable scenario for a business driven by the Mighty Dollar. As a final dampener in every sense, torrential rain flooded the roads and brought the city to a grinding halt, both physically and financially.

This was the last thing the organisers needed as they hastily tried to prepare Interlagos for its comeback as an F1 venue for the first time since 1980. While the heavily revised track was more or less complete, the same could not be said for the garage and paddock facilities. With compromise the order of the weekend, Ferrari used their red packing cases to screen off a private area for team debriefs.

When it came to protection, Jean-Marie Balestre was in need of shielding from a hostile crowd continuing to blame the FISA president for robbing their man Senna of the previous year's championship. Prost was not too popular for the same reason but, on race day, there was a new villain of the piece when Satoru Nakajima managed to collide with Senna as the Japanese

driver's Tyrrell was being lapped by the leading McLaren. A pit stop for a new nose cost Senna any hope of the victory he craved most. Even worse as far as Ayrton was concerned, Prost was now on course for his first win for Ferrari.

The victory podium made a bizarre sight, mainly because there was no one to present the prizes. Balestre, whose unquestionable right this usually was, had pushed off early without telling anyone – presumably because the thought of giving the winner's trophy to Prost would be too much for everyone to stomach, particularly the baying crowd.

As the drivers waited for the Brazilian president to act as stand-in, Prost and Senna studiously ignored each other while Berger, who had finished second, looked extremely embarrassed about it all. Prost and Nichols were the first to recognise the element of luck in a race that had unquestionably belonged to Senna but, for Nichols, this win brought a moment of quiet satisfaction in the light of an outburst from Dennis earlier in the weekend.

What do we do now? The extraordinary scene at Interlagos in 1990 as the winner, Alain Prost, and Ayrton Senna refuse to communicate while a bemused Gerhard Berger (left) looks on after the first three had waited awkwardly for someone to present the trophies.

During the course of breakfast with a group of Italian journalists, Dennis had claimed Ferrari had been able to woo Nichols by offering between $1.5 and $2 million, a figure way beyond the sum McLaren were willing to pay. Dennis then entered a more controversial area of speculation by seeming to imply that Ferrari were using bank accounts outside Italy and therefore beyond the reach of the Italian taxman. A strong denial was not long in coming, Ferrari saying their books were open for inspection at any time. The situation was diffused within days as Dennis flew to Maranello and apologised personally to Piero Fusaro, the Ferrari chairman, and Piero Lardi Ferrari, the deputy chairman. Dennis said he had answered 'a well-aimed question that had touched a sensitive spot' during the briefing with the Italian journalists. He stressed that his comments were never intended to suggest Ferrari had acted improperly. While no one doubted his words, there was also no question that the Ferrari shop floor, tied to union agreements, would now have an inkling of Nichols' retainer, much to his quiet discomfort.

Steve Nichols

I'm just a country boy and I'm not used to all this big-city stuff and contracts and politics and things like that. It's like when Prost had asked me to come to Ferrari. I went and talked to them and when they asked, 'What about the money?' I said, 'Let's talk about the job.' We sorted that out and when they asked about the money once more, we agreed a figure and I said, 'OK, I'll come.' It was as straightforward as that. There were no tricks or hard bargaining or playing smart trying to do the big deal.

So then I went back and spoke to Ron. He said, 'Don't go. Don't go.' I said, 'I'm sorry, Ron, but I've told them I'll go. I've designed plenty of cars for you. Look what happened when Barnard left – you've had plenty of chances to do something with me.' Then he asked if I had signed anything. When I said I hadn't at that stage, he said, 'Don't go. Stay where you are. Your rate card will go up.' I said that was not the answer because I'd heard that sort of thing before from him. He said to take a year off. He would pay my salary, 'but just don't go to Ferrari.' I explained once more that I'd told them I was going – so I would. He got pretty upset about it.

A few weeks later, Dennis would not have been pleased when Senna retired from the San Marino Grand Prix (a stone, trapped by the brake caliper, had machined the inside of a wheel rim and caused the tyre to deflate) and Berger dropped from first to second with an engine problem. The only consolation for McLaren was an engine failure for Mansell and fourth place for Prost – who considered himself fortunate to be there.

Alain had not been impressed by a severe case of wheel-banging as Alesi forced his Tyrrell into fifth place on the first lap. Recovering from that, Prost was later obliged to make an unplanned stop for a softer tyre, his choice of the hard compound turning out to be a rare error of judgement. There was also the small problem of the throttle slides occasionally jamming thanks to dirt kicked up by his team-mate as Nigel muscled through and forced Alain off the road during that eventful opening lap. All told, the three points were good enough to keep Prost close to Senna at the top of the championship.

I LIKE NIGEL VERY MUCH.
WE GOT ON VERY WELL
BEFORE I WENT TO FERRARI
BUT THERE WAS A SORT OF
MISUNDERSTANDING.
ALAIN PROST

Despite problems for Ferrari during most of the opening
races of the 1990 season, Prost was able to stay in
contention for the championship.

The gap would be extended by nine points when Senna won at Monaco and Prost retired from second place when the electronics affected the gear selector and then the alternator overcharged the battery to such an extent that noxious fumes filled the cockpit. When Mansell was also sidelined with an electrical problem and Williams pushed Ferrari into third place in the Constructors' Championship, it was clear there was work to be done in Maranello.

Matters appeared to be no better two weeks later in Canada when Prost was stranded out on the circuit thanks to the gearbox sensors going awry during free practice on the first day. The car held together long enough for Prost to qualify third behind the McLarens. After a cautious start in the wet, Alain did his usual trick of slowly moving forward and finding himself in third place after choosing the right moment to change to slicks on a drying track.

Unfortunately, his mechanics were not so clever. When blanking tape was not removed from the brake ducts, Prost found himself in trouble on a track notoriously hard on brakes. He managed to nurse the car into fifth place, 16 seconds behind Senna's winning McLaren. At that stage, Prost's championship chances appeared to be slipping away as he held third place, five points behind Berger and 17 adrift of Senna.

The picture would change significantly when Prost won in Mexico and France, Senna retiring from the first with a puncture and finishing third at Paul Ricard. As Prost, now just three points behind Senna, helped Ferrari celebrate their hundredth victory, Mansell was one of the few not to join in. He was unhappy for reasons other than being selected for a random drugs test.

Having led briefly, Mansell had retired with mechanical trouble. As ever, he had given his all in every sense – even sweating a couple of litres of bodily fluid when in the car. Nigel's frustration over seeing Alain win for the second race in succession would be aggravated by having to consume four litres of drinking water and wait an hour and 45 minutes in the medical centre before being able to provide the requisite sample for the drugs test. It would bring Mansell nicely to the boil in time for his home Grand Prix.

The preliminary act was played out at the end of the first day's qualifying at Silverstone (the final sessions on both Friday and Saturday counting for the grid). Climbing from his car, Mansell had a shouting match with his engineer, jumped on a scooter and barged through the group of waiting journalists, leaving these words hanging in the air, 'If you want to know what happened this afternoon, just look at the time sheet. I've nothing more to say.'

First glance at the time sheet provided few answers since Mansell was third fastest behind the McLarens, with Prost further back in sixth place. Examination of the speed trap figures, however, showed Mansell to be languishing behind his team-mate despite backing off as much rear wing as he dared.

MY FIRST YEAR AT FERRARI WAS FANTASTIC. I LIKED THE CAR AND THE PEOPLE.
ALAIN PROST

The following morning, Nigel returned to the paddock and accused the media of upsetting his team by suggesting the home hero had a horsepower deficiency. The picture became even more confused during final qualifying when Mansell turned in one of his demon laps and claimed pole. As Silverstone rose to its feet to acclaim their hero, Nigel punched the air, jumped from the cockpit and said, 'I did it for this country. The reason I'm on pole is thanks to the power plant behind me.' When pressed further by an exasperated media, Nigel admitted he may have over reacted 24 hours earlier. Whatever the description, it would be a sideshow compared to the full-blown melodrama he had in store for race day.

The sequence goes like this: Senna, on the outside of the front row, beats Mansell into the first corner. Mansell fights back, passes the McLaren, runs wide, tries again, takes the lead on lap 12 and stays there for nine laps. Then Berger takes his turn for several laps before Mansell sends the crowd into raptures with a move on the McLaren. Meanwhile Prost, hampered by gear selection problems during qualifying, has surreptitiously eased forward from fifth to second and closes on the leader – who is struggling.

Mansell's gearbox has started to select gears at random, the down shift going from seventh to fifth instead of sixth. When Mansell is momentarily delayed by a backmarker as well as being presented with the wrong gear, Prost snatches the lead to the obvious dismay of more than 100,000 fans basking in a splendid summer's day. Mentally on fire, Nigel sets the fastest lap, closes on Prost, drops back, closes again – and then rolls to a halt when the Ferrari fails to find any gears at all.

The mental flames become a devastating inferno as Mansell climbs from the car on the inside of Copse Corner. Peeling off his gloves and balaclava, Nigel throws them into the crowd. It has the hallmark of a final curtain call before his adoring fans, a view that is encouraged by a pit lane interview with the BBC in which Mansell tells his public, 'I have to be careful what I say but I just don't understand why one car is OK and mine has trouble.'

Steve Nichols

I was in charge. Nigel had a race engineer and there was another race engineer on Prost's car. I was neutral and I wanted them both to do well but the problem was that I was seen to have arrived at Ferrari with Prost. Nigel didn't really want anything to do with me because he saw me as Prost's man. His attitude was almost, 'It's me against the world – and you're the world.' I hardly worked with Nigel at all. In fact, I thought he hated me. It was only many years later when I was talking to someone about the Grand Prix Masters series in which Nigel was involved that I discovered that Nigel had recommended they hire me. Apparently, he spoke very highly of me! So, going back to 1990, it would seem it wasn't that Nigel thought I was useless, simply that I was 'with Prost'.

Nigel, Alain and I worked together that year and, while everyone talks about Prost being a politician, I never ever saw any sign of that. It was simply a case of getting the job done – and that's where the two drivers were different.

Nigel's idea of testing would be to come along, do a few laps and then do a race distance. You'd say that the test driver could do the long runs but Nigel would insist because, effectively, he could go out there, switch off and bang in the laps without having to use his brain too much. Then he'd want to do a few laps on qualifiers at the end of the day. We wouldn't have learned a damned thing.

Meanwhile, Prost's engineer would say, 'Nigel is half a second quicker than you – you've got to go out and do a quick lap.' Alain would say, 'Why? That's a waste of time. We've got to get on with our work, do a few more runs.' 'Well, Alain, you've got to do a fast lap because Nigel has done one and if you don't, the team will start to gravitate towards him because he's Il Leone and all that.' Prost would roll his eyes, ask for fuel out, qualifiers on, immediately do a lap three-quarters of a second faster than Mansell, come in and say, 'Right, can we get back to work now?' Poor Nigel would be destroyed and start to mutter about politics.

Silverstone marked Mansell's fifth retirement of the season on a day when his team-mate had scored his fourth victory. Prost walked back to the Ferrari motor home with the winner's cup to find the place devoid of media – except, of course, for the French. The rest were rushing back to the press room to file stories of Mansell's latest pronouncement. With his immensely loyal wife Rosanne at his side, Mansell had summoned the media and stood outside the motor home. He said he would see the season through, help Prost win the championship if he could and then quit. Whether or not he meant it was just as debatable as deciding whether or not Prost could become champion for a fourth time.

It did not look that way in Germany when Senna won at Hockenheim and Prost drove a conservative race to finish fourth rather than join six retirements caused by engine failure on the long straights. Senna's championship lead grew even further when he finished second (to Thierry Boutsen's Williams-Renault) in Hungary and Prost retired when locked transmission caused a spin.

There were no technical failures for Alain in Belgium. His problem was Senna on outstanding form, beating the Ferrari by three seconds to ease his championship advantage to 13 points. As Senna countered Prost's every move, that result was half-expected at Spa. But not at Monza two weeks later when Ayrton repeated the punishment on Ferrari's home turf, pole position by four-tenths marking the beginning of the rout and a 16-point championship lead at the end of it.

Throughout this increasingly tense contest between the two former McLaren team-mates, Mansell had continued to attract headlines as he softened the tone of his Silverstone speech and suggested that he might be open to offers. In Portugal, however, his actions on track would speak a language Prost did not want to hear.

Senna's desire to beat Prost in 1990 was further inflamed by Alain's Ferrari carrying the number '1' Ayrton felt he had been entitled to.

Mansell claimed pole position but a place on the front row was good enough for Prost since, more than anything, it meant he was ahead of Senna. Prost had been giving much thought to the starts, figuring that races seemed to be won by Senna during the initial drag to the first corner. Alain had spent a couple of days at Maranello concentrating solely on his start procedure. By introducing a long first gear and a short second, Prost felt he might have got the measure of Honda's power as Senna tried to come through from the second row. After that, the Ferrari's superior handling would be enough to keep him ahead. And with Mansell alongside, Senna's chances would be reduced even further.

The lights turned green and Prost could not believe what happened next. He made a good getaway but, to his amazement, found Mansell lurching across the track. Nigel would later explain that he had 'terrible wheel spin and my car got out of shape'. The two Ferraris touched, Prost's car grazing the pit wall to his right. He had to back off and, as he did so, a grateful Senna and Berger blasted through the gap left by Mansell.

Prost was seething as he found himself in fifth place. Working his way into fourth and latching onto the Senna-Mansell-Berger leading trio, a see-saw battle began as the pit stops came and went. Mansell took the lead from Senna on lap 50 of the scheduled 71. Prost demoted Berger to third soon after and was on the point of passing Senna when the race was red-flagged following an accident involving the Arrows-Ford of Alex Caffi. That was it; Prost had to accept third.

Alain Prost

I like Nigel very much. We were very close before I went to Ferrari but there was a sort of misunderstanding. He was not a good team-mate. During the whole year, I saw him maybe once or twice in the briefing. He did not want to participate.

Maybe he didn't feel comfortable because I speak Italian and he doesn't. He was sometimes a little bit embarrassed about that but we were not talking Italian all the time in the briefings. He preferred to play golf and then come back in the afternoon. That could never work well. It was as if he let me work as a No 1 when, in fact, I was not No 1. We were equal. But I was never aware of any serious problems with Nigel at Ferrari – except Estoril. I was angry then, I admit.

It was one thing for Alain to know that Senna was now leading by 18 points after the Portuguese Grand Prix and quite another to find Ayrton and Nigel the best of mates not 12 months after they had crashed into each other at the very same track. As he sat stony-faced in the press conference with the Mansell/Senna mutual admiration society to his left, Prost said he didn't want to talk about the championship. As far as he was concerned, this was more or less a dead letter with three races to go. Events in Spain seven days later would change his thinking entirely.

Senna looked on course to settle the championship when he claimed pole at Jerez. A seventh win for the year seemed less than certain, however, when Prost was 0.9 seconds faster in the warm-

up on race morning. No matter, second place would almost seal the title for Ayrton – and that seemed to be the way of it when, after leading up to the first pit stops, Senna rejoined behind Prost and appeared content to stay there.

Then, with just over 20 laps to go, the McLaren suffered a punctured radiator, courtesy of an underbody stay that had fallen off an AGS. Dennis in particular was livid with the French team for their poor preparation. Senna was not best pleased either since the championship gap was nine points with two races to go.

Next was Suzuka, scene of the Prost/Senna debacle 12 months before. The difference this time was that Prost rather than Senna

needed to win or at least finish the race in order to stay in the fight. And, once again, such tactical necessity would create controversy that would rage long after the Japanese Grand Prix was over – indeed, almost from its start.

The point about which there was no debate following the collision in 1989 was the difficulty of overtaking at Suzuka. As Senna and Prost left the pit lane line astern with five minutes of qualifying remaining, Senna knew this was the most important pole position of the season. He duly won it by 0.232 seconds on the 3.64-mile track. That was his good news.

The bad was a refusal by officials to cede to Senna's request – made the previous Wednesday – to have pole moved from the right to the cleaner left-hand side. Senna knew immediately that Prost now had every chance of taking the lead on the downhill charge to the first corner. That being the case – and recognising the superior handling of the Ferrari – Senna was also aware that his chances of winning would be reduced to almost zero. At that moment, he decided to settle the matter in the only way he felt available and justifiable in the face of intransigence by officials who, in his mind, were deliberately acting against him. That tactic would be revealed within ten seconds of the start.

Senna's predictions were confirmed first by Prost being faster in race trim during the morning warm-up and then by the red car finding more grip at the start of the race. By the time they came close to the bottom of the hill, Prost was ahead, on the left and starting to take the racing line into the first right-hander. Senna, his course set straight from the start, kept coming on the right. And coming. And coming. Photographers on the infield said there was no sound of the throttle lifting, as would be expected on the approach to the very quick entry to the long corner. A collision was inevitable. The McLaren hit the right-rear quarter of the Ferrari with such force, it snapped off Prost's rear wing and wrecked Senna's

left-front suspension. The pair, locked in combat once again, careered across the track and came to a dusty halt, deep in the run-off area. Prost immediately evacuated the cockpit. Hoping the race might be stopped, he thought about getting back to the pits for the spare car. But at the moment the officials decided neither car was in a dangerous position and the race should continue, Ayrton Senna became the 1990 World Champion. The feeling of anti-climax was immense, matched only by Prost's sense of outrage.

Alain Prost

Even knowing what Ayrton was capable of, I really was not anticipating this. That's because to do what he did, you have to stay flat [on the throttle] and staying flat is something you cannot imagine in the brain of any racing driver. I went to see his Honda race engineer to look at the telemetry. He was flat all the way. This happened in front of more than 20 cars going into that corner but Ayrton did not think about other people. He just thought about me. He was prepared to crash. After I retired from racing [at the end of 1993], Ayrton and I had a lot of discussions about many different things. But never about this.

Prost's anger at the time would be exacerbated by the absence of action by the authorities. The mood of almost disbelief would continue to the final race in Australia. Cesare Romiti, vice-president of Fiat, threatened to remove Ferrari from F1 by saying pointedly, 'We do not feel part of this world without rules.'

Ferrari were obliged to turn up in Adelaide, Prost's general sense of frustration being compounded by having to deny reports in the French press that he was on the point of quitting. His mood was not improved on race morning when, in the drivers' briefing, Ron Dennis questioned whether the tarmac inside the kerbing at the first chicane was regarded as part of the circuit (a reference to a controversial ruling over where drivers could and could not overtake at Suzuka, a decision seen by some as an attack on Senna). Prost would receive an official reprimand for walking out of the briefing, a penalty which further aggravated the situation since nothing had been said when Senna did exactly the same thing during the briefing at Suzuka.

All told, it may have intensified Prost's sullen mood but he would do himself no good in the eyes of a wider audience by failing to turn up for a photo call of world champions, Juan Manuel Fangio having dignified the 500th World Championship race by joining Sir Jack Brabham, Denny Hulme, James Hunt, Nelson Piquet and, of course, Ayrton Senna. Finishing third in the race with fading brakes seemed the least of Prost's worries as the closed season beckoned.

It was known that Alain had a second year to run on his contract but, given the edginess attending his final race, off-season rumours continued to suggest that he might quit with immediate effect. Prost neatly nailed that one in late December by agreeing to stay with Ferrari for a third year in 1992.

EVEN KNOWING WHAT AYRTON WAS CAPABLE OF, I REALLY WAS NOT ANTICIPATING THIS.
ALAIN PROST

Alain Prost

It was not one of my better decisions – although it seemed right at the time. I'd had a good year in 1990 – and good fun, too. I had won five races and was able to fight for the championship. Everyone worked very well and the ambience was fine.

It was also a clever move at the time since it squashed stories suggesting Senna and Ferrari were considering a union in 1992. Given their mutual antipathy, there was no way either driver would tolerate the other in the same team.

Any reasonable analysis of 1990 would show that Prost had done an excellent job at Ferrari, certainly good enough to demoralise Mansell to the point he accepted an offer from Williams for 1991 once the histrionic talk of retirement had been dealt with. If nothing else, Mansell's antics in Portugal – when he had come close to driving Prost off the road and had been allowed to finish ahead at the expense of Prost's championship chances – allowed Alain to express his views to the team management in no uncertain terms. A week later in Spain, Nigel had not been able to do enough for his team-mate as Prost led home their second one-two of the season. 'I have come to see,' said Alain, 'that quite often the best way to get something done is to make your dissatisfaction public.' Having had the confidence to take on the politically sensitive management in such a way, it remained to be seen if Prost could use his first year's experience to mould Ferrari into a consistently competitive team during his second term.

I WON FIVE RACES IN 1990. EVERYONE WORKED VERY WELL TOGETHER AND THE AMBIENCE WAS FINE.
ALAIN PROST

Winter testing with the 642 – effectively a revised 641 – suggested that he could. With Jean Alesi replacing Mansell, Ferrari had an interesting blend of raw talent working with a highly experienced former champion, one who had been cautious not to read too much into the encouraging off-season lap times. Unlike the team, Prost seemed to be aware that finishing one season with a winning car did not automatically mean the trend would continue. He was also mindful that McLaren – and Williams-Renault in particular – had yet to reveal their latest cars.

His concern was to be justified when Senna dominated the opening race in Phoenix with the all-new MP4/6. Prost finished second, a strong comeback from a pit stop delay proving the Ferrari was reasonable, but no more than that when compared with the McLaren. It reinforced Alain's view that Ferrari needed to produce a new car as quickly as possible. The team management, led by Cesare Fiorio, thought differently.

Policy disagreement began to become personal prior to the third round at Imola. In an interview, Prost said he was having to run the team as well as drive the car. Unfortunately, the handling of the 642 was so bad that he spun off – on the parade lap. Until that moment, Ferrari watchers believed that Fiorio's future was looking doubtful. Now the team had the ammunition to attack Prost as Alain walked back to the pits to explain why he had parked his car on the grass before the race had even got under way.

The tension was cranked up further at Monaco when Prost dropped from third to fifth following a pit stop to attend to a loose wheel. A hammer became stuck beneath the car when it was lowered from its jacks. By the next race in Canada, Fiorio had been removed, only for Ferrari to make matters worse by replacing the former Lancia team boss with a committee of four. Watching from the sidelines, Jackie Stewart was moved to comment, 'That's not going to work. It's the worst thing Fiat could have done because there's no obvious leader. And that's what a successful Grand Prix team needs; someone to say "Yes" or "No" on the spot. I can't see Alain putting up with that for long.'

The one positive move was to accelerate production of a new car, the 643 arriving in time for the French Grand Prix. Driving a largely untested machine, Prost led for several laps and eventually finished second to Mansell in the increasingly dominant Williams-Renault. Prost was among the leaders at Spa until his engine failed but took third at Monza and an equally strong second in Barcelona.

The Spanish result looked good on paper but, behind the scenes, the team was tearing itself apart, particularly as Prost felt he should have won. Lining up sixth on the grid, Alain had felt it was worth the gamble of starting with slicks on a wet track. The team management, afraid of looking foolish in the eyes of the Fiat hierarchy watching on television in Turin, had overruled their driver. Then for good measure, Alesi, starting from seventh, got into a tank-slapper as he drew alongside his team-mate, forcing Prost to back off and complete the first lap in 12th. With absolutely nothing to lose – apart from a point that was up for proving – Prost stopped for slicks after three laps. It was the correct decision – followed over the next three laps by the leaders – and sent Alain on his way to one of the best drives of the season.

Third place in Japan was better than could be expected but when asked about his car after the race, Prost compared it to a lorry. The driver had run out of patience, but then so had the management. Prost was relaxing in Port Douglas in northern Australia when he received a call telling him not to bother coming to Adelaide for the final race. His time with Ferrari was over.

Alain Prost

The first year was fantastic: in my opinion, it was my best year as a driver. I liked the car and the relationship with the people – the engineers, everybody – was really good. The only problem was the politics behind everything became a bit too much. It was really a shame that we did not win the championship in 1990. In my view, we lost it because of Nigel and the politics put together. And then, obviously, with Ayrton at Suzuka. We should have won this championship and I'm very disappointed about that because I feel that I did a fantastic job.

In October 1990, I already knew that 1991 would be a disaster. And it really was a nightmare. Not because it was the first year in which I did not win a race, but because of the politics. I don't want to go into all the stories about why they fired Fiorio and said it was because of me. I still don't know exactly why that happened because, as far as I could see, there was no reason. Technically speaking, 1991 was really, really bad. In the space of two years, you can have the good and the bad, that's typical Ferrari. It's really a shame that there are these extremes. I was experiencing a team and a country where, when everything goes well, it gives you such a lot. But when it goes wrong, it's terrible.

Maybe the mistake I made was believing I could change the mentality, the way they work and approach problems. I did change it a little bit in 1990. Then, in 1991, it changed back to what it had been. And more...

AGREEING TO STAY AT FERRARI WAS NOT ONE OF MY BETTER DECISIONS.
ALAIN PROST

Prost and Steve Nichols enjoyed an excellent working relationship.

I ended up being at Ferrari for 1990, '91 and the early part of '92. The first year was better than expected but, overall, the whole thing was such a disaster, you just wouldn't believe it could happen in a fantastic team such as Ferrari.

Unlike drivers who seem to want to race for Ferrari, I'd never really wanted to be an engineer there. But I have to admit, it did kind of get to me once I arrived. You walk into the building and there's all these sepia prints going back to the 1950s and 1960s. Photos of [Froilán] González, [Alberto] Ascari and all the heroes of the day. Like it or not, the sense of history does start to weigh on you.

Perhaps that's why such an unmitigated disaster seemed so bad. I just don't know what they could have been thinking. The engine was horrendous – I'm talking about the driveability factor. You'd come from a test and tell the engine people about the impossible driveability and they'd look at you and say, 'Well, it's not like that on the dyno.' I couldn't believe my ears. Engine people were like that back then, they're not now, of course. But in 1990–91, the engine – at Ferrari, at least – was all about one number: peak power on the dyno. You'd talk about driveability, power through the range – and you could see in their eyes that you just weren't getting through.

Alain spent a hell of a lot of time developing the engine. He was very good at that sort of thing, very good at getting the car and the engine perfect. He'd work really hard with the engineers to make the car do the work. He'd then also give 110 per cent in the cockpit and you'd be thinking, If we've got a driver of his calibre giving a 110 per cent then, with a perfect car, it's going to be fantastic. Unfortunately, the car was not perfect but Prost was really keen to make it that way. His cerebral approach was way beyond most drivers.

The problem was we'd arrived at Ferrari having come from McLaren where we were very good at developing the car and we'd won championships with a team that was doing everything almost perfectly. Take the front springs for example. At McLaren, we had the springs in 25-pound increments – that's 2.5 per cent. Normal tolerance on a spring is about 5 per cent. We had to make a whole bunch of springs and then select them within the tolerance range to make sets.

When we got to Brazil one year, Prost had the spare McLaren and he's saying that one car is stiffer than the other. I checked and they were on the same springs, but Alain was pretty sure one was stiffer than the other. I then checked the raw data – I personally had been down the back of the workshop with a press and a load cell measuring deflection and load and graphing all these springs. I looked it up and they were both ostensibly sets of 1,000-pound springs, but one was 995 pounds and the other 1,010 pounds – or something like that. A difference of 15 pounds from one car to the other – 1.5 per cent on spring stiffness – and he could feel it. Prost and Senna could feel 5 pounds downforce on the front wing, the equivalent of a bag of sugar. The really good drivers are not only able to feel the car but communicate it to the engineer.

So we arrive at Ferrari and say we want to try stiffer springs. They say they tried that. When? 'Oh, a couple of years ago.' You just wouldn't believe it. So you ask for a 25-pound stiffer front spring, only to be told that Ferrari's springs are in 250-pound increments. They're going to jump straight over the sweet spot! OK, so how long's it going to take to make some? 'Oh, about three months.' It was a totally different way of working.

The thing that didn't change was Alain's way of working. You could go testing and make any suggestion you liked: 'OK, Alain, we're going to put the front tyres on the back and the back tyres on the front to see if that gets rid of the understeer.' He'd say, 'OK, I'll give it a go,' and go out and do five hard laps. That was his work ethic. It was his dedication to the cause and that never changed despite what was going on around him in 1991. I think the parting of ways was inevitable.

The rumours, ticking over gently, suddenly accelerated the moment officials removed the name 'PROST' from above the door of the Ferrari garage in Adelaide. Being early November and late in the negotiating season, Prost's options for 1992 were limited. But that did not stop the speculation. He was, after all, a triple world champion with 44 wins to his name. At times like this, however, logic takes a back seat, as was shown when conjecture started again almost before the Christmas recess was over.

If the location was unlikely, then so was the story. Reports in the first days of January from Uruguay said Prost had signed for Benetton, the source being no less than Luciano Benetton, as he opened a clothing store in Punta del Este. This was a surprise, not least for Michael Schumacher and Martin Brundle, already in possession of Benetton contracts for 1992. It was true that Prost had spoken to team boss Flavio Briatore. But he had also held exploratory talks with Williams and others.

Alain Prost *When I was in Australia, in Queensland, on the way to Adelaide in 1991, I had a call from the Elf people. We started to talk about the '92 season and they were telling me that maybe they would have the opportunity to replace Nigel at Williams. To be honest, I didn't know what to say. On the one side, you are happy because people are interested in you. But, on the other side, it would not be good to be in the middle of a polemic like that. I said we should wait until we got back to Europe and we would see what happened. It took a week or two before they told me it was not going to be easy. I said I could understand that and I was talking to other teams about 1992.*

The rumours continued, a plausible suggestion being that Alain might join Ligier. The story gained legs on Sunday 19 January when a driver wearing plain white overalls and a helmet belonging to Erik Comas was seen to do 49 laps at Paul Ricard. Anyone close enough would have recognised the familiar bridge-of-the-nose profile through the helmet slot, the game being given away completely when the car stopped out on the circuit and the slightly built driver emerging from the cockpit most certainly was not Comas.

This was to be the start of serious discussions that would run until the week before the first race in South Africa on 1 March. Renault were interested in committing to engine supply for at least three years but, in the end, Prost and Guy Ligier, although remaining good friends, could not find an agreement.

Alain Prost *It was obviously too late to find a really competitive car for '92, so I said, 'OK, I'm not going to be World Champion. I'll go this way and try to build my own team.' During the winter Guy Ligier and I talked for a long time and the deal came very close to happening. For me, it was very important to have stability in the team, so I wanted a five-year deal, to be secure. It was only a technical problem. I felt this was necessary to be competitive and to have enough money to get the right people to do the thing properly. But, for Guy it was different, selling the team in the right way, and so on.*

If I was going to have my own team, I wanted it to be based in France and using a French engine. But I never liked the idea of setting up a sort of l'ecurie France *– a French national team – as such. In the end, we couldn't find the right solution for us both. There was no problem with Guy. But we weren't fooling ourselves. If we couldn't get the money needed to take the team to the top level, then why do it? So I decided to have a year off and prepare myself mentally and physically for winning the championship in 1993.*

As far as my driving was concerned, I wasn't worried. I had a lot of parameters for that and I'd like to think I'm quite honest with myself. My team-mate in 1991 had been Jean Alesi, who was very young, very brave and very quick. If I'd been a second slower than him and struggling a little bit, I would have retired. Immediately. But I was quicker than him, so that had been a point of reference.

Prost's testing had also provided a point of reference for Frank Dernie, the former Williams engineer working with Ligier at the time.

Wearing a crash helmet belonging to Erik Comas, Prost prepares to test a Ligier at Paul Ricard.

Frank Dernie

I was astonished when Prost tested with us. Knowing his reputation, I wasn't really surprised by the quality of the feedback he gave us; I was ready for that. But what did surprise me was how quick he was. However great a driver he had been all those years, for some reason I never really thought him as ultimately quick, in the 'Senna' sense of the word. Which was a bit silly, given his record. He was really fast. Very impressive indeed.

Meanwhile, Prost was already looking ahead to 1993.

Alain Prost

When it became clear that nothing could happen with Williams for '92, I said that maybe we could think about 1993. That led to a discussion with Renault and Elf and Frank. I don't remember when exactly we agreed on making something happen, but it was around the time the 1992 season started.

As the season got going and Mansell began a run of five victories in the Williams-Renault FW14B, speculation about Prost's future died away, only to be reignited in June when he turned up in Montreal to commentate for French television. His sabbatical was clearly doing him good.

'Everyone tells me I look years younger,' he told a group of journalists. 'Maybe. I don't know, but I feel it. Physically, I feel better than for a long time, because I'm half on holiday all the time. A lot of golf, a lot of cycling. I always had fun around the sport and at the moment I have time for it.'

When asked about his future plans, Prost said, 'I admit I was completely fed up with the Ferrari situation last year. I felt... tired, you know. I really needed a break. In the end, I finally have my year off because I don't have a car to drive. But maybe that's a good thing. Maybe I would never have done it otherwise. For now, I'm with friends, having a nice time. I don't worry too much if it's one o'clock in the morning because I know I can wake up at 11 if I want. All these years I've never been able to do that and it's really a different life. At the moment I don't want to think too much. I just want to relax, to be more... quiet. But I know I can't do that forever.'

Prost did admit that he had maintained contact with Williams, but allowed that Frank had to be primarily focussed on the 1992 championship.

With Mansell clinching the title in Hungary on 16 August, Frank could then enter into serious discussions. 'Serious' in this instance had several strands. Mansell was running a hard-nosed negotiation over a renewal of his contract for considerably more than Williams felt he was worth despite Nigel's new status as world No 1. (Claiming money was not the issue, Nigel said, 'It's only tenth on the list.' To which Frank famously murmured, 'Hmm. It is the list!') Senna, meanwhile, was destabilising the entire process by suggesting he would drive for nothing, a measure of how far the Brazilian was prepared to go in order to keep Prost away from what was clearly the most competitive car in the field. Frank Williams, ever the pragmatist, had thought from as early as the start of the season that there were few downsides in hiring a three-time World Champion who was popular with Renault, devoid of contractual complexities, free from hang-ups – and ready to start immediately. At a press call at Estoril on Tuesday 6 October, the name Mansell and the Union Flag were removed from the flank of a FW14B and replaced with 'Prost' and the French tricolore. Officially, Alain Prost was a Grand Prix driver once more.

Not so fast, *monsieur...*

Time to relax and enjoy life in 1992.

On 12 February 1993, at a restaurant in London's Greek Street, a letter from FISA president Max Mosley to Frank Williams was revealed at a press lunch hosted by Martin Brundle and Mark Blundell. The fact that the journalist with the letter was not prepared to divulge his source was almost as controversial as its contents and overshadowed, with the greatest respect, anything either of the Ligier drivers had to say.

In the leaked document, Mosley roundly condemned Prost's attitude to Formula 1 in general and FISA in particular. Mosley had been angered by comments made by Prost during his role as TV pundit in 1992, followed by further caustic remarks in a French motoring magazine. In a long interview Prost said that F1 was being badly managed and without consultation. Judging by the tone of the letter, Mosley was not best pleased.

'We really have to ask ourselves,' wrote Mosley, 'if the best interests of Formula 1 and the FIA World Championship are served by allowing a man like this to participate. He clearly thinks he should be running everything. He pontificates about things he does not understand and he described the entire governing body in contemptuous and offensive terms. He even attacks Formula 1 for being too concerned with money when he had probably taken a bigger share than anyone, certainly more than the members of the FISA World Council, who earn nothing.

'I do not believe,' Mosley continued, 'that you or your sponsors can control him. Indeed, I am sure you have clauses in your contract which cover this situation but have had no effect. Even if he cannot be quoted directly he will probably find a way to poison the atmosphere just at the time we most need to improve it.'

Prost would later show that the printed words in the magazine had little connection with the actual audio tape of the interview, although he did not feel the need to comment on the alleged critical remarks made during commentary. In the meantime, Bernie Ecclestone was adding fuel to the fire. Referring to Prost's sabbatical, the vice-president of promotion affairs at FISA asked, 'Do you think it's right that someone like Prost can play around with Formula 1 the way he has in the last year? He has created enormous problems for his team, he simply disappeared whenever he pleased, spent a year lazing about and then demanded a crazy sum of money. Prost has been doing what he likes in Formula 1 and we'll have to have a word with him about that.'

Even allowing for Ecclestone's penchant for mischief-making, the implication of Mosley's letter was that Prost would not be granted a Super Licence.

Alain Prost *I always felt the support from Frank and Patrick. I didn't understand what was happening at the time. It looked like maybe some people were not very happy for me to come back. Even now I cannot say why but I definitely had a problem with the FIA maybe not giving me a licence.*

That threat hung in the air until the teams assembled at Kyalami for the first race on 14 March and was not answered until Prost started practice along with the other 25 drivers. And won pole. And the race. It was the first of seven wins, laying the bedrock for a commendable fourth World Championship. Yet Prost's achievements throughout the year would carry a weary hint of dissatisfaction in the media, as if prompted by Mosley's strident pre-season criticism.

Prost took the first of seven victories on his return to F1 in South Africa.

WE HAD DIFFICULTIES WITH THE CLUTCH AND THAT DIDN'T HELP AT DONINGTON.
ALAIN PROST

Few could argue with his performance in South Africa but the same could not be said for the next two races. He started from pole and led in Brazil until a misunderstanding over a radio message meant Prost stayed out a lap too long as the rain came down and he understeered off the road on slick tyres. During the European Grand Prix at Donington Park he made no less than seven pit stops due to constantly changing conditions, the majority at the wrong moment for the wrong tyre. He finished third, one lap down, his performance seemingly made worse by a mesmeric drive from Senna in the winning McLaren-Ford.

Not long after the finish, Williams aggravated the situation further by questioning Prost's judgement. Frank's remarks were seized upon by the media, notably the French press. Two days later, Williams and Renault inadvertently drew more attention to Prost's plight by issuing an excruciatingly stilted defence of their driver. As public relations exercises went, it was an unmitigated disaster and did nothing for Prost's peace of mind.

As if that was not enough, Prost also found himself in trouble on a totally unexpected front.

Jean-Louis Moncet

Alain said to me, 'I have a big problem.' Naturally, I thought he was talking about the car or something that happened in the race at Donington. But it was nothing to do with that. Lady Diana [Princess of Wales] was at this race and she had met Alain somewhere before. She was one of the last people to leave the grid. Alain was on pole position and, as Lady Diana and her bodyguard walked by, she... how do you say... caught Alain's eye. So he waved back. The next thing there is a big casino [fuss]. The president of Renault received a letter to say what Prost had done went against royal protocol and they requested an apology. This was done without hesitation, of course. Alain was about to start a Grand Prix. He had no idea he had done something wrong!

Adrian Newey (above, left) and Patrick Head worked closely with Prost during a year that brought five victories, including Canada (right, top) and Germany (right, bottom).

Prost did not put a foot wrong in the next two races at Imola and Barcelona, despite having to nurse his car home on both occasions. The San Marino Grand Prix was blighted by the throttle jamming open at random, the active suspension then occasionally going awry and giving Prost a rough ride in Spain. But neither of these technical setbacks would create such offence as the stop-go received for jumping the start from pole at Monaco. Prost felt the penalty was heavy-handed and ruined any chance of denying Senna his record-breaking sixth victory in Monte Carlo.

People remember 1993 as being 'easy' for me. But a lot of things had been happening. We had difficulties with the clutch that year and that didn't help at Donington. In Brazil, I was on my way into the pits when my engineer started to talk over the radio. In fact, he was saying there was a lot of standing water in the pits and that I had to be careful. But the reception was terrible. I guessed there was something wrong and, in a split second, I had to decide whether to continue coming in or do another lap. I made the wrong choice.

But the Monaco penalty was very bad. At the start I had taken first gear and the car had started to move a little. The stewards told me afterwards that I had the penalty not because of a jumped start but because the car moved – and that is not allowed. But what I found difficult to accept was being penalised when a lot of drivers were not for doing the same thing or even worse – and not only at Monaco. I had the feeling that someone wanted to make an example of me.

At the 13th attempt, Prost finally managed to add Canada to his victory roster, following it up three weeks later with his sixth win in France. That result gave Williams their first one-two of the season as Damon Hill dutifully followed home his team leader – but only after Hill had led from his first F1 pole and a slow pit stop had allowed Prost into the lead. As far as certain members of the British media were concerned, Hill had been denied his first win after having served his time as test driver for Williams before being made a member of the race team for 1993.

It was perfect newspaper fodder on the eve of Silverstone the following weekend. The expectant crowd came close to witnessing the dream result when Hill, getting the jump on Prost's pole position sister car, led for 41 laps. Then his engine blew, just as Prost was pressing hard after an earlier struggle to get by Senna's extremely wide McLaren.

This was Prost's 50th Grand Prix win. Not that you would have known it judging by the muted reaction. Hill being robbed of victory was part of it. But an underlying cause was the continuing belief that Prost had eased Mansell out of not only Williams but also F1 and sent him packing to Indycar in North America. It was a notion that received short shrift from Frank Williams and his technical director, Patrick Head.

Patrick Head *It was absolute nonsense that Prost manoeuvred the situation, shafted Mansell and so on, as was suggested by certain sections of the national press. Obviously a lot of that came from Mansell himself and I thought it was pretty smelly stuff, frankly. But, of course, people believed whatever they wanted to believe.*

Alain Prost *I must say, I found it a bit strange. I had won at Silverstone ten years before and got a great reception. And that was when I was driving a Renault. I won my first championship in England [at Brands Hatch] and, even though that had been Nigel's first win in F1, I still got a big cheer. Even when I won at Silverstone in the Ferrari after Nigel had retired, it was the same. But the win in 1993 was... different. I think it was*

because of everything that had happened with Nigel and the fact that he was the reigning world champion but he was not racing in front of his fans.

Hill's patience appeared to pay off at Hockenheim. Having led every lap, the Englishman had it made as he backed off the revs and made the most of a ten-second gap over Prost with two laps to go. Then he suffered a left-rear puncture –

and Prost inherited the win. Alain's mixed emotions were compounded by a penalty for deliberately steering his car into the escape road at the Ostkurve chicane on the opening lap. Had he not done so, Brundle's spinning Ligier would have taken out the Williams. Prost's presence of mind had earned a stop-go, not to mention a growing and understandable feeling of persecution.

Hill would finally score his maiden win in Hungary on a day that Prost stalled at the beginning of the parade lap and was forced to start from the back of the grid. After working his way into the top six, Alain then suffered a breakage in the main beam supporting the rear wing. When he came into the pits for a replacement, Prost suffered a further delay while the mechanics were forced to stop everything and take part in the pit-stop routine as Hill

arrived for fresh tyres. Prost eventually rejoined and set the fastest lap on his way to 12th place, seven laps behind the winner.

It may have been nothing to write home about but, in adversity, Prost had quietly gained a few admirers. One of them, Les Jones, was No 1 mechanic on Hill's car.

Damon Hill (above, left) joins Prost, Newey and Head for lunch. Alain discusses the Williams FW15C with his engineer, David Brown (left on right-hand picture).

Les Jones

When we had to stop work on Prost's car, he just sat there, calm as you like. There were no hysterics. When the wing was changed, he went back out and really drove hard until the end. He finished 12th, which is nothing. Some drivers I know would have given up the minute they came into the pits. I'd no real feelings either way about Prost, to be honest. I mean, he was Damon's main competition! But, I tell you, he really earned my respect that day.

Hill would go on to win three in succession. At the third, the Italian Grand Prix, the boot was on the other foot in the sense that Prost was leading and heading for the win that would secure the title when he suffered his single engine failure of the season when 15 miles from home. Prost completed the job in every sense by finishing second two weeks later in Portugal – having announced his retirement from the cockpit earlier in the weekend.

To the outside world, the news was surprising on several counts, not least for the suddenness of the press conference, held in a stuffy room above the pits in Estoril and prompted by a French radio station taking a gamble and announcing the news prematurely. Here was a driver, racing for the best team and walking away from the chance of winning a fifth title to equal Fangio's record at the time.

Prost admitted he had an enjoyable relationship with the team, got on extremely well with Hill and seemed genuinely pleased when Damon won a race. He had clearly earned the respect of his team. And yet he was leaving. The journalists present could see the name 'Senna' written between the lines of platitudes about 'this being the right time' and 'quitting while ahead'. For once, the speculation was correct.

Alain Prost

In the middle of 1993, we had discussions about Ayrton coming to Williams. That was difficult for me. Never, at any time, did I ask to be a No 1 or a No 2. The only thing I said to Frank was you are not going to have Ayrton in the same team. Some time later, Frank called me. I knew already from a few weeks before that Williams were having some pressure from Renault to have Ayrton. I was in the south-west of France and Frank said he would come to see me.

I always remember this day. He said, 'I have pressure, what can you do? How do you see these things? What do you think?' I said, 'If you want to take Ayrton, you choose. I want to compete against Ayrton – I have no problem about that – but not in the same team. I want to fight on the track. I want to have the best chance possible to beat him on the track. You know that.'

So Frank had to make a decision. I did not ask for stupid money. I did not ask for anything. The reason I did not want to be in the same team was for one reason. At McLaren, I had been doing 80 per cent of the tests. When Ayrton was tired, he went back to Brazil and, when he was doing a test, I was doing promotion work. I told Frank that he couldn't put me in this situation. Then I said to Renault, 'OK, you are pushing for Ayrton and you gave me aggravation this year because it is not easy. I have a two-year contract. You pay me the second year of my contract and I leave.' And that's exactly what happened. I knew then that 1993 would be my last season even though I did not want to stop.

It had been a difficult year. I felt very well inside the team but, outside the team, it was a very strange ambience with the press. When you looked at the press in France, when I was winning it was absolutely normal because I had the best car and I was with the best team, more horsepower than Ayrton's car – and things like this. Always, always a polemic; it's very difficult to motivate yourself when it is like this.

It was black-and-white all the time. When you lose a race like Donington, people do not realise there are many, many reasons for this. Ayrton's car in the wet, technically, was a different car. For sure Ayrton was very fast but, in those conditions, his car was much better. Winning is one thing, but you need to win in a good ambience.

At Imola, I realised there was no objectivity because I'd had a good win despite problems with the car and nothing was said. Then you have a race like Donington and some guys immediately

write that you're finished. Then you win the next weekend and you're fantastic. That's what I didn't like, the way you were rated only by your last race. Some of the best drives are in races you don't win. Any driver will tell you that.

But, as I said, I very much enjoyed racing for Williams. I had a really good relationship with the team and a big, big admiration for Frank. I worked well with Patrick – even though he could sometimes say things that were... very direct! Obviously Frank is Frank, Patrick is Patrick. I liked them both because they are competitors even if they are different. Frank is a manager. Patrick is more passionate about the technical side. But the great thing is they both want to win.

Sir Frank Williams

Nigel was Nigel and drove brilliantly for us. Alain was a very different human being. He had enormous talent but he was also very easy to get on with, very straightforward. He was incredibly smooth and precise. I remember we had a sort of running joke where I would tell him to let me know when he was going for pole because otherwise I would miss it. Saying that, I thought his drive at Barcelona was terrific. His car wasn't working well at all and his pole lap there was sensational. It wasn't a Prost lap as we had come to know it because it showed he could hang it out if he had to.

Patrick Head

Prost didn't have the need to be dramatic, which was why his winning always came across a bit clinically. Whereas Nigel would operate on an emotional basis, Alain was more intellectual. In some ways, I'd say Alain was a bit enigmatic for us. I'm sure he wasn't like that at McLaren but he'd had this experience of feeling he'd been pushed out of McLaren by Senna. So, he came to us and won the championship – but it was almost like he came and he went. He walked in this door and he walked out the other door and we never really knew him. He and his engineer, David Brown, worked closely together but I'm not sure that even David knew him. We didn't really get to know the personality of Alain Prost.

Prost and Frank Williams enjoyed a straightforward and productive partnership in 1993.

The start of a new phase in their relationship as Senna raises Prost's hand on the podium at the end of Alain's final Grand Prix.

Decisions and announcements may have been made for the future but the 1993 season still had two races to run. When Prost finished second to Senna at Suzuka, Ayrton froze him out completely, shunning a handshake on the podium and barely able to mention his name in the subsequent press conference. When asked if he would bury the hatchet at Prost's final race in Australia, Senna mumbled, 'Maybe. We'll see.'

The answer to that question was going to come whether Senna liked it or not as the pair repeated the result in Adelaide. The world watched with interest as the leaders completed their slowing down lap, Senna stopping, as had become his habit, to pick up a Brazilian flag. *Parc fermé* was in a garage at the end of the pit lane, officials slamming the doors shut once the McLaren and the Williams had rolled to a halt.

For a couple of minutes, the two men who had dominated the previous decade were alone. Prost had completed his last Grand Prix, Senna had brought a very successful six-year association with McLaren to a perfect conclusion.

Prost climbed from the cockpit, removed his gloves, helmet and balaclava and then walked to the back of his car before squatting down to examine the rear diffuser. A few feet away, Senna took longer to vacate the McLaren. Neither driver acknowledged the other's presence, the relative silence after an hour and a half of noise intensified by every movement echoing within the barren garage.

Ron Dennis arrived and embraced Senna, congratulating the Brazilian on his fifth win of the season after yet another immaculate performance that had as much, if not more, to do with the driver than the car.

Then Dennis walked over to Prost and put his arm around the Frenchman. There was genuine feeling here. For six years they had worked together while Prost brought McLaren three World Championships and 30 victories between 1984 and 1989. It was clearly something neither side would forget. Senna, meanwhile, kept his distance.

As Prost headed towards the door, he passed Senna and they shook hands. There was very little warmth. But, as far as these two were concerned, it amounted to something of a breakthrough. Once on the rostrum, Senna grabbled Prost's wrist and pulled him onto the top step, where they embraced. It brought an instant response from the crowd. Newspapers the following day would speak of Senna's generous gesture.

A cynical interpretation of the moment was that Senna was calling the shots once more, knowing Prost would not dare to refuse the hand of friendship in such a public place. The last thing Prost needed was to be seen making his final exit as a sad figure rejecting Senna's overtures.

The bottom line, however, was that Alain Prost was no longer a threat in the eyes of racing driver Ayrton Senna. That moment on the podium would indeed mark a major turning point in a relationship that had held the world of sport in its thrall.

ALAIN PRO

4ème

TITRE

13. THE THIRD SENNA

Damon Hill (left) and Ayrton Senna at an Estoril test at the
start of a difficult relationship with the Williams-Renault FW16.

Prost had barely time to hang up his helmet when the phone rang a few days after his final race in Adelaide. It was Senna. Receiving such a call was akin to Boris Spassky ringing Bobby Fischer in 1972 for a chat about life in general. The tense contest between the two greatest chess players in the world was the ultimate sporting metaphor, one which became a clash of superpowers as the American challenged Spassky – and, in effect, Russia. The thought of these two men from very different cultures sharing friendly words would have seemed as unlikely as Senna admitting Prost existed, at least until that moment on the Australian podium on 7 November 1993. Even then, there was the inescapable feeling that Senna was making the first move towards checkmate.

Alain Prost

When we reached the podium, I did not want to say anything. For me, the season was over, my racing career was at an end and so was the fight with Ayrton. But from that moment, the whole thing changed. Completely. He got me to stand on the top of the podium. After what happened at Suzuka, I really wasn't expecting that. But if that was a surprise, the press conference was unbelievable as he talked about our racing in a nice way. It really seemed genuine although, as you can imagine, I was a little confused. I was to discover that it really was sincere when he called me two days later and told me some very personal things. Did we become friends? That's difficult to tell but, for sure, we were to become very close. However you wanted to describe it, our relationship was obviously very different compared to what it was.

As 1994 got going, Prost looked on and listened with interest as Senna swapped his familiar Marlboro McLaren overalls for the blue-and-white of Rothmans Williams-Renault. This was the first time Ayrton had changed teams in six years. Apart from the need to settle into a new environment, he also had to quickly come to terms with the realisation that the latest Williams was not as good as everyone expected it to be. Senna as championship favourite may have been a common theme in season previews but it added to the pressure.

The more Senna became aware of the matter-of-fact predictions, the harder he tried and the more difficult the Williams FW16 appeared to become. Designer Adrian Newey had miscalculated the effect of a major change in regulations that wiped out the active suspension and other gizmos that had previously made the Williams unbeatable. Instead of being comparatively easy to drive, FW16 was edgy and unpredictable. Proof of that would come when Senna spun in front of his adoring fans during the first race of the season at Interlagos.

DID WE BECOME FRIENDS? THAT'S DIFFICULT TO TELL.
ALAIN PROST

Three weeks later, the Pacific Grand Prix had barely started when Ayrton was forced off the road at the first corner at Aida in Japan. His feeling of frustration was not improved as he watched from the trackside and felt certain that Michael Schumacher's Benetton-Ford appeared to be employing traction control, one of the many devices supposedly banned.

A second win in succession for the German meant he had gathered 20 points. For Senna, it was the first time in ten years that he had got this far into the season without finishing on the podium. He hadn't even scored a point. The Williams appeared to be getting no better, Senna's unfamiliarity with such a dire situation being summed up by his team-mate.

Damon Hill *In the team – and I understood this – I was the understudy and I didn't have a problem with that, given that I was 33 when I got the opportunity. I was really grateful to be there. Ayrton was very different to Alain. He needed to win and he was fighting with a car that was difficult to drive in the sense that racing cars can sometimes be difficult to drive. It wasn't a beautiful experience to drive that car. It was a classic Adrian Newey car – no knuckles left. You had scabs on the knuckles from being scrunched up in there. It wasn't quite set up right, having gone back to passive suspension, so it was tricky to drive. Ayrton, being new to the team, was asking me, 'Is this normal?', and I'm saying, 'Well, I'm relatively new here as well. I was hoping you'd be able to tell us!'*

With Schumacher in the ascendant, Senna arrived at Imola knowing
he somehow had to stop a precocious driver nine years his junior.
With the sort of superhuman effort only Senna was capable of,
he put the Williams on pole for the San Marino Grand Prix. But
even that had little or no significance for Senna as he struggled to
come to terms with the death of the young Austrian driver, Roland
Ratzenberger, during qualifying. It was the first F1 fatality since de
Angelis in 1986.

Prost's opinion was keenly sought to discuss matters such as Senna's failure to score
points in the first two races of 1994 (Above left).

Ever since Adelaide, Ayrton had become a new person. A new driver, also. He said he had lost his motivation, lost his goal, his objective. He explained all this to me. The strong person in the car just disappeared. I was completely surprised and astonished about this change which, he said, was because I was not there any more as a competitor.

In the week before Imola, he even said a few things to me about his personal life that I will never tell anyone. He told me in confidence but I could never ever quite understand why he told me these things, even though they explained a lot about him. He opened his heart about his problems and his personal life.

He explained that our battle on the track had been very important but he said he was not motivated to race against these guys [in 1994]. Again, I was very surprised. I had never been able to understand how he behaved as a racing driver and now I could not understand 100 per cent how he behaved as a human being.

On the Sunday at Imola, not long before the race, he came up to where I was with some Renault guests and we talked for about five minutes. Once again, I was surprised because it was very strange just before a race for any driver to do that – never mind Ayrton. Then he went back to the Williams garage. I went there too, and that was my last moment with him. He was talking about things he was not very happy with about the Williams and also

the Benetton which, in his view, was not completely legal. In effect, he was showing himself to be in a weak position before the race. This was definitely not the Ayrton I knew from the past – this was a completely different Senna.

The outside world received only a hint of this when the television camera showed a preoccupied Senna sitting in the cockpit of his Williams on the grid. For once, he did not get out of the car, preferring to sit, helmet and balaclava off, lost in his thoughts. Over his right shoulder, on the outside of the front row, sat the green-and-blue Benetton he wanted to beat more than any other car on the grid. That's what the world at large believed. Prost was one of the few to have other ideas about Senna's primary motivation after their private discussion not long before.

Schumacher had been 11th fastest in the morning warm-up, suggesting he would start the race heavy with fuel (mid-race refuelling was allowed for the first time since 1983). That would appear to have been a ruse when the Benetton slotted in behind Senna and stayed with the leading Williams on the charge through Tamburello and on towards Tosa. By the time they started the downhill plunge to Acque Minerali, red flags told of the chaos that had erupted on the starting grid seconds after the green lights had come on.

Ayrton Senna's Williams-Renault leads the Benetton-Ford of Michael Schumacher on that fateful day at Imola in 1994.

Alain's presence as a pallbearer at Ayrton's funeral said
much about their relationship. Prost is joined by Emerson
Fittipaldi (left), Gerhard Berger (right), along with Christian
Fittipaldi and Jackie Stewart (behind Prost).

Prost, working for the French television station TF1, would have been asked to comment on Finnish driver JJ Lehto stalling and the Lotus of Pedro Lamy, starting from the back of the grid, smashing into the Benetton. He would also have remarked on the appearance of a safety car – then a relative novelty in F1 – to control the field at slow speed rather than stopping the race altogether. The painfully slow procession went on for four laps before the hopelessly inadequate Opel saloon safety car pulled into the pits.

Schumacher continued to hound Senna as they completed another lap at racing speed and set off for the seventh time towards Tamburello. As Senna reached 193 mph, the Williams failed to follow the accepted line through the long left-hander. Less than two seconds later, the car hit the concrete wall lining the outside of the corner.

Prost and fellow commentators, aghast at what they had seen, were left to make sense of Senna's sudden departure from the racing line and, even more difficult, the possible outcome. A helicopter shot showed the Williams to be upright but without its right-front wheel. Senna remained perfectly still in a cockpit which, to all intents and purposes, looked intact. The immediate thought was that he would climb out and walk away. Safety in motor racing had improved immeasurably. And yet there was the lingering thought that Ratzenberger had died the previous day.

Alain Prost *You don't know what to say. It's a big accident but then you think about Gerhard [Berger] escaping after his car caught fire and Nelson [Piquet] having a big shunt at Tamburello and being okay. But you really can't make a judgement because you have no facts. Then you think about Ratzenberger and about Ayrton and the conversations I'd had and the Ayrton I'd seen not long before and his motivation being different. All these things are going through your head and you have to be very careful what you say. You are very confused.*

Ayrton was taken away by helicopter and the race restarted. You have your job to do. It was very difficult because the rumours began, some saying he is dead, others that he only has a broken shoulder. Once again, you don't know what to say. And, meanwhile, there is a race going on.

Everyone's worst fears were confirmed after the race had finished. Alain was on board a chartered plane to Paris with the president of Renault when word came through that his former team-mate, rival and newfound friend was dead. He felt sick to the pit of his stomach.

Alain Prost *Some people were eating and drinking. I could not eat... I could not talk. You can imagine all the things going through your head after the unbelievable experiences since Adelaide and the things I had learned that weekend.*

I had to decide what to do about going to the funeral in São Paulo. I wanted to be there, obviously, but I did not know if I would be welcome and I did not want to cause a problem for his family or anyone. They would have enough to think about without that. I called Jean-Luc Lagardère, the president of Matra. His Brazilian wife would know what the situation would be like. She said I should do it. I was not very confident at the time but, looking back, it was one of the best things I have ever done. It was a finality, a closure. I was a pallbearer, which meant there was no misunderstanding about our relationship. It was a day of big emotion. I'm very happy to have done it.

Senna's life and death would spawn many books and a documentary, *Senna*, that focussed on his racing career using archive footage and home video clips. In the absence of formal commentary, the thoughts of family, friends and colleagues provided the backdrop for this evocative movie. *Senna* received critical acclaim and, among several honours, the World Cinema Audience Award for a documentary at the Sundance Film Festival.

The film, for obvious reasons, concentrated on the rivalry between Prost and Senna. However, motor sport insiders who knew both men felt uncomfortable with the good-guy/bad-guy theme and the imbalance created by the lack of a reasoned conclusion. This was not the Prost they knew. And, as Alain wished to relate but was not given voice on the film, it was not the Senna he knew in the final few months of Ayrton's life.

Alain Prost

I had got to understand more about how he was. I already knew a few things, learned quite a lot from the family – about how he was when he was young and that kind of thing. I knew how he was in F1 at the beginning and, obviously, with me both as a competitor and then a team-mate – and everything that happened after that.

But when we talked after I retired, I discovered the way he was thinking was unbelievable. He had made much of his career, his motivation and thinking, only about one person. Me.

I could talk about some of the things he did when we were racing but there is no value in that any more because I can now understand why he was like this. It's because he was different. And when he explained everything, I began to understand just how different he was. His story suddenly had much more meaning.

I have seen a big part of the film. I'm disappointed rather than upset because there is only one opportunity to make a film like this and that moment has now gone. When they first talked to me about the film, they asked if I wanted to be part of it. I said, 'Sure. Why not?' The only condition

– well, it was not a condition but you need to understand I told them, 'It would be fantastic if you could show the Ayrton before he arrived in F1. What he was like in F1, fighting with me or against me and the Ayrton after I retired. If you do that, a mix of the nice stories and sport, even when it's hard, the fight and the human side then it's going to be a good film. Because this was really something unbelievable. In my opinion it is a fantastic story. But you need to mention a lot of things that happened after I retired.'

I did almost eight hours of interviews. Eight hours, talking much more on the human side so that you could understand how he was before he came to F1, how he was when we were racing and how, when I retired, there was a new Ayrton Senna – a third Ayrton Senna. It is a fantastic story in sport, one that only happens, I don't know, four or five times in 50 years. Even if it finished badly for Ayrton, it is really a nice story at the end.

AYRTON WAS THE BEST DRIVER I EVER COMPETED AGAINST.
ALAIN PROST

But what I do not like at all in the film is that this did not come across. I find it very bad and sad. If they wanted to do a commercial film with the bad guy and the good guy, then do not make any interviews, do not ask me anything. But as I said, in the interviews I did with them, I was trying to explain all the things that happened before Imola when Ayrton called me – not every day, but almost.

At Imola, Ayrton had recorded a film with Elf in which he was supposed to drive round and say things about the track through a microphone in his helmet. Ayrton began by saying, 'I would like to say welcome to my old friend Alain Prost. Tell him we miss him very much.' I found this out when the guys from TF1 – who were using the film – showed it to me. It was a nice moment.

So, in the film Senna, you can hear the bit where he says he misses me. But, as I have explained, there was much more to it than that. In the film, they completely miss the point. The reason I could not be happy was not because I looked the bad guy. I don't care much about that because... I'm alive, I'm OK. But I would like everyone to know who Ayrton Senna was, what exactly our fight was about and also what happened at the end.

If you want to tell a story, tell the true story, not just that very short clip from the car. The thing I wanted to explain, to see in the film, was that Ayrton was a different person when he was fighting against me. He was different to when he was fighting against Michael [Schumacher] or Nigel [Mansell] or whoever. And then there was the Senna at the end – the third Senna. That was so important – and it did not come across in the film. The point is, our story did not end in 1994. Our story will last forever.

Dave Ryan *The Senna film was wrong. But, typical Alain, he didn't start shouting and saying, 'That's crap! That's not how it was.' They invited a few of us to a viewing in London. I watched it and I didn't feel it was right. It wasn't the final version. When people asked me if I was going to see that, I said I didn't want to watch it again because it's not the full story. People who weren't around at the time would come away thinking that's how it was... which is very unfair and completely wrong.*

The 1986 championship contenders – Senna, Prost, Mansell and Piquet – before Ayrton moved to McLaren and Alain would have felt less inclined to put an arm around his shoulder. The same could be said for the Williams drivers when their relationship came under strain a year later.

Stefan Johansson

I didn't think they did a good job at all. I actually met the director because I did some work for them in Sweden when they launched the film. I said I'd worked with both Senna and Prost and, at best, it was six of one and half a dozen of the other. As far as I was concerned, Alain had not come out of this very well. It was not a true reflection of the guy I knew and for whom I have so much respect. They didn't do Prost any favours whatsoever.

Jean-Louis Moncet

All of the film is to the glory of Ayrton. Alain Prost is the bad boy. That was not correct at all. Only at the end of the film do you see Alain with the coffin in São Paulo and there was mention of the film clip we used on TF1 of Ayrton at Imola saying he missed his friend Alain. But, other than that, nothing. This is not the right impression of how it was between Alain and Ayrton during that short time in 1994. When the Air France jumbo landed in São Paulo at the time of the funeral, a helicopter came alongside and took Alain to see Ayrton's family. He was the only driver to see the family. That was part of the big change in the relationship between Ayrton and Alain but there was nothing to say this in the film. That was very bad.

Tim Wright

I thought the film was very one-sided; that's why I didn't want to see it again. Obviously, there were a lot of evocative clips in there – especially at the end. But the image they created of Prost really upset me. How can you tell people things weren't like the film portrayed? It just wasn't like that as far as Alain was concerned.

Steve Nichols

I never did get to see the film and, from what I've heard from people whose opinions I respect, I'm glad I didn't. To suggest that Prost is a conniving bastard – which I believe the film does – is simply not correct. He's not like that – at all. Everyone talks about Prost the politician. I never ever saw even the tiniest little bit of politics. At McLaren or Ferrari, whatever the year, it was always the same with Alain: just get the job done. I had enormous respect for them both. I'm just happy I was lucky enough to be around when they were both racing. And it's good to know Alain feels the same way, despite everything that went on.

Alain Prost

Even after all this time. I always get the same thought and feeling that I had in 1994 – but not in 1993. You cannot talk about the human side of the relationship when you are competing with each other. In any case, as I said, it's not my intention to speak any more about what happened between us on the racetrack. It's the overall picture that's now important.

Ayrton was the best driver that I ever competed against. He was the best because he was different. It was almost frightening the way he was able to impose himself on everyone. The way he worked, he was able to get something more from the team and from the people working with us. With Ayrton, it was not just what he did on the track because we all know that he was very good on the one lap. Very good. But he also had this concentration and focus on using the full potential of the car, the tyres: everything. I was never convinced a hundred per cent that he was good at setting up the car but, overall, he was the best; no question.

Most important, however, is that I'm so pleased I had this relationship with Ayrton after I retired. It helped me appreciate and understand just why he really was the best.

AYRTON MADE MUCH OF HIS MOTIVATION AND THINKING ONLY ABOUT ONE PERSON; ME.
ALAIN PROST

14. GOOD MAN - BAD CHOICES

Prost chats with Gianni Agnelli, the head of Fiat and Ferrari, during an ambassadorial role with McLaren-Mercedes which also included the thought of a comeback and test drive in 1994 (right).

In July 1995, Prost made a rod for his own back. Interviewed by Benetton Formula's race-by-race magazine, Alain explained that he was filling his days as an ambassador for Renault, spending time with Anne-Marie and their sons Nicolas and Sacha and playing golf.

When asked, 'What puts you in a good mood?' Prost replied, 'It's easier to list what puts me in a bad mood. I don't suffer fools gladly and I don't like stupidity or work that has no purpose. Turning the question around, I'd say that being with interesting, capable people puts me in a good mood. So does taking a project all the way through to fruition.'

That last line was poised to haunt him over the next seven years. Within weeks of the interview, Prost and Renault had decided to part company, Prost stressing it was simply 'au revoir' and a mutual agreement that would allow 'my career to have a fresh direction'. This prompted anticipated speculation over his future, columnists noting that, with Renault's approval, Alain had tested a DTM Mercedes. His name also continued to be linked with driving a Renault Laguna in the French Touring Car Championship.

In the background, though, were hints that Prost continued to think about a French F1 team. Indeed, discussions with Guy Ligier had picked up where they had left off in 1992. It was no surprise when, in early 1997, Prost completed the purchase of Equipe Ligier, the team that, somewhat fortuitously, had won the Monaco Grand Prix the previous May. Olivier Panis, the French driver on that emotional day for France, would stay onboard what would be known as Prost Grand Prix.

With the season upon them, there had been no time to design and build a new car, Prost relying on the latest Ligier powered by a customer Mugen-Honda engine. It served them well, Panis finishing on the podium in Brazil and Spain. Despite the euphoria, Prost had been round the block often enough to recognise that F1 was rarely that simple.

And so it would prove. Not many weeks later, Panis broke both legs in a heavy shunt during the Canadian Grand Prix. Although only a novice, Jarno Trulli stepped up to the plate and showed remarkable composure by actually leading the Austrian Grand Prix until the engine blew up. When the Italian finished fourth in Germany, Prost had seen enough to have Trulli join the recovering Panis for 1998. And, for good measure, Prost would have a contract with Peugeot for the exclusive supply of engines. This deal, with the under-performing and unreliable V10, was the first of several bad choices, one of the many strands that contributed to the team's ultimate downfall. The 1998 season almost failed to get under way thanks to trouble passing the crash tests. It ended with Prost Grand Prix at the bottom of the championship with a single point.

There was a step forward in 1999 when Trulli finished second in Germany. But that would be the only decent result in a season of unfulfilled promise. The decline from here on would be rapid and painful despite the presence of Jean Alesi and Nick Heidfeld, backed by an impressive roster of commercial partners ranging from Gauloises to Yahoo and PlayStation.

The financial backing gradually disappeared thanks to a recession made worse by uncertainty in the aftermath of the September 11 terrorist attacks in 2001. On top of which, the increasingly tenuous relationship with Peugeot finally collapsed, leaving Prost to race Acer-badged Ferrari engines for a variety of drivers in 2001. Further disagreements, accidents and more bad choices did little for Prost's peace of mind.

RUNNING A TEAM WAS THE MOST STRESSFUL TIME I EVER HAD – BY A LONG WAY.
ALAIN PROST

On Monday 28 January 2002, the Tribunal de Commerce in Versailles placed the company in liquidation with debts of more than £10 million.

As Prost stood outside the courtroom, he looked pale, drawn and somehow even smaller than he actually was. He openly admitted that the tribunal's decision was, in one sense, a release from a relentlessly bruising experience. No one doubted that he had put his heart and soul into the project, working until 11 pm each night and putting out many fires – even if, in some cases, they could have been avoided in the first place.

Prost had been getting barely enough sleep through worrying about the team and the many talented individuals gathered under his roof. And that was another problem. Prost had moved from Ligier's rural location to a state-of-the-art headquarters in Guyancourt on the outskirts of Paris. The 75,000-sq-ft offices and factory may have been only 20 minutes from Orly airport and an hour from Charles de Gaulle airport, but the location was simply another expensive wrong choice.

As a team leader, Prost had bad breaks and went down technical cul-de-sacs, but the series of poor decisions and an inability to delegate merely proved that a top sportsman, selfish through necessity, does not necessarily make a sound businessman. Commercially, Prost was out of his depth in a pool famously populated by piranhas.

Alain Prost *I didn't really want to run a team in the first place. I knew it would be very, very difficult in France but I was being pushed by the French politics to do it.*

Considering all the aspects, I think we didn't do too badly. The relationship with Peugeot was never good because they did not want to put in any money. Then I had signed a very good contract with Yahoo but we could not do it because of an internet crisis [bursting of the dot.com bubble]. I had also signed a contract with [Saudi Arabian billionaire] Prince Alwaleed to buy the team for his son – then we had 11 September. And so on.

I don't want to go too much into detail but we were paying $28 million for the engine. We were supposed to pay $32 million the year after. If you look at what happened to Brabham and Jaguar and other teams and what was happening with the economy in France, what can you do?

I suffered because the image was not that good. In fact, I thought it was a good experience. The only thing I regret is that we needed one more year to prove that we were much better than it looked. In any case, finding the right money to continue would have been very, very difficult.

It was the most stressful time I've ever had – by a long way. I was happy when we stopped because you cannot do that for ever – work with no consideration for anything else and just attack. My telephone was red hot. I was leaving the factory very late every night. In some ways, yes, this was a failure that I had to accept. But my thoughts were with the team, a really good team, the best I could put together. But I received so many blows for months and years that, in the end, the court decision was almost a relief.

Prost remains supremely fit, largely through his passion for cycling. Alain poses with legends Eddie Merckx (left) and Bernard Hinault at the Tour of Oman.

After running his F1 car (top right), Prost returned behind the wheel and scored many victories in the Andros Trophy ice racing championship.

Prost focussed on cycling, his skill and a return to full fitness bringing pleasure and success in French events. The need to compete also led to ice racing and repeated victories in the Andros Trophy. The latter satisfied his continuing love of driving while further ambassadorial work with Renault and commentary for TV station TF1 perpetuated the link with F1. In 2014, Prost became involved with Formula E through assembling a team for his son Nicolas who was following in his footsteps as a driver.

It is an almost impossible act to follow. Regardless of what Alain does now or in the future, nothing can diminish his place in motor-sport history and the memory of such a distinguished career.

Alain Prost

People have this 'thinker' image of me, The Professor, as I'm sometimes known. I'm actually quite pleased with that even though sometimes in normal life people who are thinking too much are considered boring. But that's the way I am and I can certainly live with it.

I'm aware that I have a kind of sensitivity when driving the car. I don't know where it comes from. I've always enjoyed that feeling of control. I remember, when I was racing in F3 and everybody had a seat, I wanted to sit on the aluminium monocoque just to feel the car.

I'm very tactile. I like to touch and you'll notice that I use my thumb and forefinger a lot when trying to explain something. I'm like Ron in wanting things a certain way. When I was in the car, I didn't like it if I broke a front wing. It wasn't my car, not my money and it could be repaired but I still felt very bad.

That's why I did not want to do the 24 Hours of Le Mans when I had some offers because there would be three drivers and I really didn't want to share the car. I like to have my objects. I like to touch. I would say to the mechanics, 'Please clean the car perfectly. I want to enjoy getting into it because it's nice and clean.' It's not the sort of thing you can explain. You don't learn it – you either have it or you don't.

When you feel things like I did [in the car], sometimes it can be a disadvantage because, even if it's a little problem, you think about it and you are not so confident. But when everything goes the way you want then, for sure, you are better. Which is why I always had better fuel consumption and less wear on the tyres, why I would brake less. That is also part of the way you are. That's why different attitudes and ways of driving are part of the history of F1. We are all different. I am me – and I'm happy with that.

Saying that, I've been involved in controversy from time to time. Again, I can live with that because I really don't think you can have a career of 15 years and more without controversy. You know that one day it will happen – and, if it doesn't happen, nobody remembers you anyway so I think it's more positive than negative.

I've been very lucky, too. I've had some accidents, as racing drivers do, and all I've had is a fractured wrist [in 1980]. Before that, I'd never hurt myself in motor racing despite a few big crashes. As soon as you have a physical pain, it makes you change completely. Even a little pain makes you think differently, but it did not detract from a fantastic career working with some really great people.

Indy Lall

I look at Alain in two different ways; as a professional sportsman and as a human being. I took to him very much because, I have to say, he almost seemed vulnerable. Not that you wanted to mollycoddle him, but he was a very sincere guy who sometimes looked as if he needed an arm around the shoulder. Ayrton was just pure emotion and you couldn't help but love that too. When you think about everything that happened between Alain and Ayrton, first and foremost it was between two very competitive human beings and it was a natural thing. Whether it was with us at McLaren or the pair of them in two different teams, the same thing would have happened.

Alain was an absolutely genuine guy. He is shy and would rather lean towards people he knows and trusts. He had insecurities, just like everyone else. It was painful to watch the way he would bite his fingernails! But you couldn't help but warm to him. And, at the end of the day, he did such an amazing job on the track. In fact, there was a point when it looked like he might be racing for us again in 1996.

Given his friendship with Ron [Dennis], Alain was willing to rally to the cause in case Mika [Hakkinen] was not able to come back from the injuries he received during the 1995 Australian Grand Prix. We even went as far as having a test with Alain. He was wearing neutral overalls and the thing I remember was Jo Ramírez [team co-ordinator] doing a really neat job covering the markings on Prost's helmet with white fablon. It was too good a job because, when Jo went to remove the fablon afterwards, he found his work with a scalpel had scored and completely screwed Alain's helmet!

In the end, of course, Mika was able to come back so Alain didn't need the helmet anyway. But it was nice working with him again, even if just for a couple of days. Overall, I've nothing but good memories of working with both Alain and Ayrton.

Ron Dennis

Alain and I were always close friends – and still are. I can't remember the circumstances under which he drove our car but without question it was with a view to seeing if he would return to Grand Prix racing. And again, when Mika was injured, we considered Alain driving for us as an option in '96 because we continued to have such a good relationship.

Prost and Ron Dennis continue a good relationship beyond Alain's six seasons with McLaren.

Neil Oatley

Alain was a little bit political but he wasn't as overtly emotional as Ayrton, which is probably why Senna was a bit more widely loved outside the team. It's like the old saying about the American drivers, AJ Foyt and Parnelli Jones: Jones would do almost anything to win and Foyt would do anything to win. I think that also applied to Prost and Senna.

Dave Ryan

What was really nice about Alain was that he's a proper Frenchman. He'd arrive in the morning, go round everyone, shake hands, say, 'Good morning,' spend ten seconds chatting to each one and then move on – but without it seeming like he was just going through a process. It was like he was genuinely interested. Even when things weren't going well, he never failed to do that.

The frustration that he must have felt in the later years – the problems he was having with Senna and all the rest of it – that never overflowed into the garage; it was always contained in the motor home or wherever. That's how it appeared to us. So, in that respect, he was just a really good guy to have around.

He seemed to be a great team player to the guys in the garage. Unlike modern drivers who have this 'I couldn't have got any more out of the car today', Alain was often quoted on the podium as saying 'A monkey could have driven this car today, it was just so good'. He was very quick to praise the team when things were going really well. He made known it wasn't all him – obviously, it was – but he would be quick to spread the credit around.

Steve Nichols

Prost was the most normal guy that you could imagine, kind and gentle, polite and considerate, friendly. Just a regular guy. The only oddity in his personality or his character, whatever you want to call it, was that he was freakishly good at driving a racing car! Otherwise, nothing abnormal at all. He was not a diva or a prima donna, superstar or anything like that. Just a nice guy. And still is.

Of course, I think that went against him when he tried to run his own team. Because you're a good racing driver doesn't necessarily mean you're going to be able to run a team and all that entails from the business and, particularly, the political aspects – the sponsorship hunting and so on. That's just a different mindset and a racing driver doesn't necessarily have that. It works both ways, of course. Ron Dennis: brilliant team manager, but put him in a racing car? Why would you? Nobody would think to do that and yet they'll take Prost and tell him he can run a F1 team. It doesn't work like that, as Alain found to his cost.

Neil Trundle

As you know, when Senna was around, there seemed to be a hell of a lot going on behind the scenes but Alain never complained about politics. He never bitched to us. Mind you, the car was usually pretty good, so there was no reason. But he was always such a gentleman, always nice to the guys. He never made a mistake, never went off. The perfect driver from a mechanic's point of view.

Tim Wright

Alain was a pretty motivational guy. He could be political but that never came in to the working relationship he had with us. He kept that to one side. Obviously there were occasions when he was wound up by certain things but he never let that interfere with getting on with the driving and understanding the car. He was very good with the guys, always said, 'Good morning,' and 'Cheerio and thanks.'

We socialised quite a lot. He and Jacques Laffite had a golf course near Dijon and one of the nicest things we ever did was take part in a golf tournament there. Not that I was any good but it was a nice gesture to be asked two years running.

Alain enjoyed his golf. When testing was much more relaxed and there was a problem at Monza – something to do with trees in a run-off area and the drivers refusing to go out – he went off to play on the course close by the track. It took hours to sort this out and I remember having to go and try to find him when we needed him. He was such a relaxed character.

PEOPLE HAVE
THIS 'THINKER'
IMAGE OF ME; THE
PROFESSOR AS
I'M SOMETIMES
KNOWN. I'M QUITE
PLEASED WITH
THAT.
ALAIN PROST

Jean-Louis Moncet

My admiration for Alain is not just because he was a good driver, a World Champion. In 1980, his apartment was in Saint-Chamond, not in Paris. He was, how do you say, a redneck. In French we say a 'plouc'. Fourteen years later, we are having lunch together and he is meeting with the Queen and the British ambassador in Paris to receive the OBE. Louis Schweitzer [Renault chairman] was also there. I remember looking at him and thinking how far he had come from being a redneck. I really admire him for that but mainly because he has not changed. Not at all.

Ron Dennis

You could argue that perhaps Alain has not received the respect he definitely deserves when people talk about the great drivers in F1 history. Part of that is because he was understandably very French-centric and didn't really invest much time outside the French media. And also, his private life was colourful and that dampened some of the perception people had of him in France. His relationship with quite a few members of the press could be described as low-key. That, in turn, meant the media would fuel that and force him to push towards only making sure things were portrayed in France in the way he wanted them to be. That created a sort of negativity in the rest of the world, but it certainly didn't bother me or anyone on the team.

The simple fact is that Alain won three World Championships with McLaren. That obviously brings many vivid memories, such as driving down the Champs-Élysées with thousands of people lining the route, police outriders, the whole thing. It was a magic moment.

There were so many hilarious practical jokes and fun behind the scenes. There was good humour most of the time in the team. One of the challenges of being a team principal is that sometimes you have to be tough and that can make life more difficult. But it's helped a great deal when you've got a good personal relationship such as the one we had. I also think Alain appreciated McLaren much more after the period running his own team. It was certainly a wake-up call in respect of what it took to make and run a competitive team.

There were moments when I think both of us would have done things differently. But that's inevitable when you have someone staying with the team for such a long time. The bottom line is that, by and large, we had one of most successful driver/team combinations in the history of motor racing – and we're still good friends at the end of it.

YOU COULD ARGUE THAT PERHAPS ALAIN HAS NOT RECEIVED THE RESPECT HE DEFINITELY DESERVES.
RON DENNIS

Alain Prost

I can only have good memories of my time with McLaren. In fact, I did think about going back in 1994. When I announced my retirement at Estoril near the end of 1993, Ron called me – I remember very well, I was in the hotel – and he asked why I was stopping. He did not know this at the time but he said he had the feeling that I didn't want to stop and he wanted me to come back to McLaren. I said if I stop, I stop. I can't leave here and then go back. But he kept insisting.

During the winter, I had many, many calls from Ron. When you stop, you start to feel you are missing something. I said to Ron that I was a little lost. I also wasn't sure about the Peugeot engine [McLaren were making the switch from Ford to Peugeot for 1994]. He was offering a big deal. I said, 'I tell you what we'll do, we'll have a contract for three days. I'll test at Estoril and after the three days I'll tell you what I'll do.' He paid me, but it was not about the money, it was the principle. After a day and a half, I said I'd finished my job. I'd been happy to do it – but I didn't want to come back. That was very good for me to have done that.

Saying that, I had some difficult times at McLaren. But we should not forget that I was working with the team in 1995. I was very happy there and one of my few regrets is that I left McLaren in 1996. As I said, I bought the Ligier team mainly because the French government pushed me a lot. It put an end to discussions Ron and I were having about what we could do together. One of the ideas we had was for me to have a McLaren team in America.

McLaren was like a family and, as with any family, you cannot always have just the good things. We had a very difficult situation in 1989 that we haven't exactly forgotten – but it's almost a joke now, even if it was very tough at times.

Looking back, I cannot regret anything. The only thing I regret is the bad accidents involving many of my friends. I'm so happy that I never really hurt myself. If I had to do it again, I would not change anything.

INDEX

Alazar Trophy 29
Alboreto, Michele 103, 120, 121, 123, 124, 127, 131, 133
Alesi, Jean 240, 244, 257, 303
Alexander, Tyler 46, 49, 57, 100, 319
Alliot, Philippe 170
Alonso, Fernando 15, 209
American Motors 72
Andros Trophy 306
Argentine Grand Prix 72
Arnoux, René 72, 75, 76, 79, 80, 81, 83, 84, 88, 90, 153, 170
Ascari, Alberto 261
Australian Grand Prix 133, 136, 158, 162–5, 169, 184, 206, 228, 232, 240, 255, 259, 281, 285, 288, 308
Austrian Grand Prix 93, 136, 153, 303
Autodromo Municipal de la Ciudad de Buenos Aires 72

Balestre, Jean-Marie 21, 61, 72, 81, 116, 232, 243
Barnard, John 66, 69, 99, 100, 109, 115, 121, 141, 145, 150, 153, 155, 165, 180, 240, 319
leaves Ferrari 224, 244
leaves McLaren 170, 173
BBC 248
Beaumont, Marie-Claude 54, 57
Belgian Grand Prix 59, 83, 103, 131, 202, 250
Bell, Bob 209, 222, 319
Bellof, Stefan 106
Benetton, Luciano 264
Benetton magazine 300–1
Berger, Gerhard 110, 145, 169, 170, 177, 201, 214, 240, 243, 244, 247, 251, 291
Bhat, Eric 45, 46
Blundell, Mark 268
Bousquet, Jean-Louis 43
Boutsen, Thierry 148, 250
Brabham, Jack 96, 141, 255
Brands Hatch 90, 93, 106, 120–1, 134, 149, 274
Brazilian Grand Prix 54, 57, 59, 72, 83, 87, 100, 103, 120–1, 131, 141, 173, 189, 190, 194, 214, 243, 261, 291
Briatore, Flavio 264
British Grand Prix 146, 198, 228, 239

Brown, Creighton 197
Brundle, Martin 264, 268, 275
Buenos Aires Autodrome 52
Button, Jenson 12

Canadian Grand Prix 223, 247, 258, 273, 303
Champs-Élysées parade 116
Cheever, Eddie 88
Clark, Jim 96
Clearways 133
Cogan, Kevin 46, 49
Concorde Agreement 72
Constructors' Championship 45, 136, 247
Coulon, Jacques 43
Cudini, Alain 38

Dallest, Richard 38
Daly, Derek 59, 84
Danielson Renault Europe 38
de Angelis, Elio 52, 81, 103, 106, 116, 120, 124
death of 142, 145, 150, 165, 287
de Cesaris, Andrea 72, 124, 223
de Chaunac, Hugues 43
de Lautour, Simon 18, 21, 22, 40, 319
Dennis, Ron 66, 69, 96, 97, 99, 104, 109, 115, 116, 130, 133, 142, 146, 150, 162, 165, 180, 183, 206, 214, 217, 218, 221, 222, 227, 228, 243, 244, 253, 281, 307, 308, 313, 314, 319
Depailler, Patrick, death of 62
Dernie, Frank 264, 267, 319
Detroit Grand Prix 124, 145, 146, 174, 177, 193
Diana, Princess of Wales 271
Dijon-Prenois circuit 36, 38, 75, 76, 80, 104, 106, 310
Dix, Glen 165
Donington Park 65, 270, 271, 273
drugs tests 247
Dumfries, Johnny 142
Dutch Grand Prix 45, 62, 79, 80, 88

Ecclestone, Bernie 45, 268
Estoril circuit 109, 110, 115, 134, 177, 189, 206, 228, 239, 252, 267, 277, 314
European F3 Championships 43
European Grand Prix 270
European Junior Championships, 1973 29

Fabre, Michel 26
Fangio, Juan Manuel 11, 255
Fédération Internationale du Sport Automobile (FISA) 21, 61, 72, 76, 79, 80, 87, 116, 232, 240, 268
Ferrari company 11, 49
Ferrari, Piero Lardi 244
FIA World Championship 268
Fiorio, Cesare 257, 258
FISA World Council 268
Fischer, Bobby 285
Fittipaldi, Christian 45
Fittipaldi company 45
Fittipaldi, Emerson 112
Forghieri, Mauro 83
Formula 1 (F1):
commercial agreements 72
drivers' strike 142
in Eastern Bloc 153
Goodyear returns to 75
Goodyear withdraws from 72
politics within 61, 80, 255, 268
tragedies strike 80, 83, 84
turbocharging rises within 87
tyre problems 161, 183
youngest-ever driver 15
Formula 2 (F2) 43, 46, 66
Formula 3 (F3) 43, 44, 45, 46, 49, 66, 100, 142
Formula Atlantic 46
Formula E 306
Formula One Constructors' Association (FOCA) 61, 72, 76, 80, 87
Formula Renault Europe 18, 36, 38, 40, 43, 45, 46
French Grand Prix 75, 84, 104, 149, 193, 198, 247, 258, 273
French Touring Car Championship 301
Fullerton, Terry 29
Fusaro, Piero 244

German Grand Prix 62, 80, 150, 174, 201, 224, 250, 303
Giacomelli, Bruno 59, 81
Gilles Villeneuve circuit 124, 223
go-karting 25, 26, 29–30, 54, 142, 156

ACKNOWLEDGEMENTS

I am greatly indebted to Alain Prost for his support and time given over to discussing and answering questions about such an interesting and significant life.

I am also very grateful for the help of Nigel Moss, Matt Bishop and especially Steve Cooper of McLaren Racing for their valuable enthusiasm and support.

As ever, this book would not have been possible without the vital contributions from members of McLaren Racing, past and present, who took time to pass on their personal memories of working with Alain. Thanks to: Tyler Alexander, John Barnard, Bob Bell, Ron Dennis, Mark Hannawin, Tony Jardine, Indy Lall, Gordon Murray, Steve Nichols, Neil Oatley, Dave Ryan, Peter Stayner, Neil Trundle and Tim Wright.

Thanks also to: Paul-Henri Cahier, Frank Dernie, the late François Guiter, Sir Patrick Head, John Hogan, Darrell Ingham, Stefan Johansson, Les Jones, Linda Keen, Niki Lauda, Simon de Lautour, Nigel Mansell, Jean-Louis Moncet, Keke Rosberg, Sir Jackie Stewart, John Watson and Sir Frank Williams.

Maurice Hamilton

Bibliography

Alain Prost Competition Driving, by Alain Prost (Hazleton Publishing)
Life in the Fast Lane, by Alain Prost and Jean-Louis Moncet (Stanley Paul)
Autosport; *Autocourse*; *Motor Sport*; *The Guardian*; *The Independent*; *The Observer*

Published by Blink Publishing
107-109 The Plaza, 535 King's Road,
Chelsea Harbour,
London, SW10 0SZ

www.blinkpublishing.co.uk

www.facebook.com/blinkpublishing
twitter.com/blinkpublishing

ISBN: 978-1-90582-598-1

A CIP catalogue record of this book is available from the British Library.

Design by www.envydesign.co.uk

Printed and bound in Poland by Interak

Colour reproduction by Aylesbury Studios Ltd.

1 3 5 7 9 10 8 6 4 2

McLaren © 2015
Text written by Maurice Hamilton 2015
Text © Blink Publishing

Pictures selected by Blink Publishing

Papers used by Blink Publishing are natural, recyclable products made from wood grown in sustainable forests. The manufacturing processes conform to the environmental regulations of the country of origin.

Blink Publishing is an imprint of the Bonnier Publishing Group
www.bonnierpublishing.co.uk